Changing Times
SERIES

GRIMSBY
remembered

Taken before the amalgamation of the Cleethorpes and Grimsby transport undertakings in January 1957, this postcard view of Old Market Place deserves close inspection. The postcard cost $3\frac{1}{2}$ d from a bookshop in Chantry Lane.

Changing Times
SERIES

GRIMSBY
remembered

Compiled by
Brian Leonard

TEMPUS

Tempus Publishing Limited
The Mill, Brimscombe Port,
Stroud, Gloucestershire, GL5 2QG

ISBN 0 7524 2466 1

Typesetting and origination by
Tempus Publishing Limited
Printed in Great Britain by
Midway Colour Print, Wiltshire

Steam trawlers moored in the Fish Dock.

Contents

'A railway line used to cross the river just there' said Harry Leonard. His great, great granddaughters (pictured) were more believing than his grandson Brian had been.

The Beasley family in September 1949: Fred and Elsie with Mary, Joan, John and Monty the dog. Their ironmongers shop provided a wide variety of essential household goods.

Introduction

'Home Town,
Want to wander round your back streets,
See your tumbledown old-shack streets,
I'm going back to see those corny country cousins of mine.

I see an old schoolhouse door
Where we used to tumble through at four,
There's a small candy store
Where I could go a dozen lollipops and shout for more'.

Words sung by Bud Flanagan and Chesney Allen that evoke much nostalgia. The song, by Michael Carr and Jimmy Kennedy, was recorded on 9 October 1937, and triggers memories of streets long gone, old buildings, as well as our school days (good or bad!) and those favourite shops we loved to visit.

For me, interest in Grimsby's past began on Boulevard Avenue bridge over the River Freshney with my granddad, Harry Leonard. He was a real leg-puller, renowned for teasing. He looked towards the Boulevard and told me that a railway line had once crossed the river and football pitches. At nine, I wanted to believe him, but when I looked for evidence, there was none. Suspecting another leg-pull, I didn't challenge his statement.

The story stayed with me, and some forty years later I found an 1889 Grimsby map. I was pleased to find the railway line marked, just where granddad had said. Its tracks led to the Alexandra Docks. As the Boulevard recreation ground was established, and houses in the Joseph Street, James Street and Lancaster Avenue area were built, all traces of the line disappeared. More recently, see how Peake's Parkway has removed all evidence of the direct London railway line, especially at the Weelsby Road junction.

Incidentally, I have been unable to find a photograph of that old railway line. Can anyone help?

I recall a 'tin' (corrugated iron) chapel nestling below the Garden Street signal box during the fifties. It was painted very dark, possibly green. Whilst compiling a study on Great Coates for my college course, I spoke to an old gentleman in that village. He recollected that a tin chapel had once stood at the corner of Woad Lane and Station Road, near to Great Coates level crossing, but it had been moved to Garden Street. For years I could find no support for his story, until recent investigation revealed that 'in 1895 the Primitive Methodists set up an iron chapel' in Great Coates. This structure was moved in its entirety from Woad Lane to King's Terrace (Garden Street) in 1945. It replaced a similar one built as an off-shoot of George Street Methodist Church in 1913, which had been bombed and destroyed. In 1965 the ex-Great Coates building was finally demolished. Again, photographs are scarce. Had not the Great Coates resident casually passed on the story, another bit of history would have been lost.

Cleveland Bridge is still with us, but not carrying the traffic of its heyday. As a child, seeing it almost daily, I often wondered why there was a second bridge over nothing. The whole long structure would have been constructed when the tramway was built in 1912 to carry Grimsby workers to the new Immingham Dock. A friend suggested that the Great Central Railway had intended to build a locomotive servicing depot on the field nearby, and the second bridge was to allow rail access. Another suggestion was that a farmer on the river side of the bridge needed access to the field near the school, and the bridge allowed him to move his cows. What was the real reason for the second bridge being built?

Interest in our past seems to provoke more questions than there are answers. George Morton recently recalled the visit of the Cadbury's Chocolate Train in the early thirties. He can just remember going with his father to the East Marsh sidings behind the Albert Gardens near Dock station. The train was in silver livery, and each child received a bar of Cadbury's chocolate. However, what was the exact date, and which engine pulled the coaches? My brief search revealed nothing, but George is convinced that the information will be stored somewhere. Can you help?

Compiling this book has brought many fascinating stories to light: memories of Dobson's the ironmongers, the Ploggers, another singer called Bing, living with a disabled father after the First World War, and so many more.

I hope this book brings you some memories of streets, buildings, school days, shops and other facets of life gone by. Perhaps you will be encouraged to write down your own memories and pass them on to your family, as some of my contributors have. Only in that way can we preserve our past, celebrate our present, and look forward to a better future.

Acknowledgements

Many people have encouraged the compilation of this collection of memories of my Home Town. Their support has been very much appreciated. The pictures are mostly from personal collections, though photographs on pages 22, 93 and 119 are by kind permission of the *Grimsby Telegraph*. The people to whom I am grateful include Jean Ashling, Marjorie Barron, John D. Beasley, David G. Bradley, Patricia Bradley, Phyllis Chapman, Betty Clark, Ken Craggs, Norman Drewry, David Edwards, Betty Fox, Stanley Gilleard, Barry Hall, Anne Harris, Peter Hewitt, Annie Hewson, Derek Hill, Don Holmes, John Hutton, Sandra Leonard, Ivy Maidens, Roger Marsh, Terry Miller, George Morton, Lorna Osbourne, Linda Oxley, Sue Pannell, Jim Parker, Doreen Phillips, Owen Riggall, David L. Riggs, Eileen Riggs, Ellie Roberts, Eric Robinson, Geoff Rudd, David Sellers, Alan Smith, Keith Smith, Chris Stephens, Maureen Thompson, Joyce Tyson, Connie Ward, Ernest Watson, Enid Webb, Joyce Wilkinson, Norman Wilkinson, Betty Williams, Doug Wise, Ray Woods and Linda Wright.

I am especially grateful to my old friend John D. Beasley, author of several other books in this series, who pestered me into compiling this book. John kindly read the original typescript and the proofs, and has made many helpful suggestions. I am also indebted to David G. Bradley for his valued help in researching and checking the details, and with several other tasks.

CHAPTER 1
Home Life

David Bradley 'digging for victory' in his parents' Sutcliffe Avenue garden in 1942. Note the Anderson shelter in the garden next door.

Keeping Food Fresh

Before refrigerators were used in most homes, milk, cheese and some other foods would go bad very quickly in hot weather. Housewives bought perishables more frequently in those days as grocery stores (corner shops) could be found every few hundred yards.

However, to extend the life of many foods, people used their ingenuity to keep food cold. To start with, it was always stored in the coldest place in the pantry, out of direct sunlight and low down. The cleverest idea was to store it on something that would drain heat out of it, a slab of solid concrete on the floor. In our house this 'gantry' was the width of the pantry, under the big shelf by the window, and the gantry was about six inches higher than the floc Dad tiled ours. The life span of all food k on this gantry was longer than that ke any of the shelves.

A milk bottle cooler. The instructions read: 'Immerse in water and drain.' As the water evaporates from the pot, heat is drawn from the bottle inside, so cooling the milk.

Cold meats were kept in a 'safe', but it had no lock! The one my Aunt had was typical. It was a simple cupboard about eighteen inches high, with wooden top, bottom, sides and back, but it had a wire gauze panel in the door to deter entry by flies. Its effect was limited to preventing flies from laying their eggs on the meat, but when there was nothing better, it was a valuable asset.

Ray Woods

Lens in the Back Garden

¹ World War, as people
'ives, food was still
buy. Mindful
be self-suffi-
nickens or even

rabbits to help out the diet. Chickens were the favourite because, whilst they were growing bigger, they produced eggs. These were a luxury during the war, when the only form of egg for many people was the dried variety. It might have been satisfactory for cooking, but everyone agreed that you couldn't eat it any other way.

Many people kept a few birds in a run or shed in the back garden. There were two popular breeds, Rhode Island Red and White Leghorn. The former laid brown eggs, the latter laid slightly smaller, white eggs. There was no difference in taste.

The birds were bought as day-old chicks, and my dad used to collect them from the Grimsby Town railway station on his bike. At home in the shed, he had prepared a covered cage, heated by a 60 watt bulb in a tin with cloth around it. As the chicks grew, the heat was gradually withdrawn, until the birds could go into an inside chicken run, before being put outside. They were fed on corn, but to keep the cost down they were given boiled potato skins mixed with 'chicken meal', a beige powder which coated the potatoes and provided extra nutrients. The birds were fattened up for Christmas or Easter, when they were sold. Meanwhile, their eggs added a treat to the weekly diet or a boost to the family purse.

A fresh, young and tender chicken for the holiday was a special treat for many families struggling on limited rations, but not many people were able or willing to prepare the birds for cooking. People who were able to do this were highly respected for their skills. Locally, that task fell to our neighbour, Mrs Hobson. She would prepare dozens just before Christmas, often sitting just outside her back door plucking off the feathers. She was able to do everything else that was necessary to make the birds 'oven-ready'. One of her perks was to keep the eggs that were forming inside the hens.

In the late 1940s and early '50s, my dad had in the garden four separate chicken runs, which must have accommodated over sixty young birds. As they grew bigger and needed more space, one or two would disappear from time to time, and we had chicken for dinner again. We may not have had much other meat, many sweets or much fruit, but we were never hungry.

Brian Leonard

Our first Television

We got our first television when I was nine, just before the Queen's Coronation in 1953. It was a Rentavision set, and I remember when the men came to install it. The first programme we saw was 'Meet the Penguins', a children's cartoon, but it was upside down until the engineers sorted it out. The first 'soap' I remember was *'This is the Grove Family'*. It was really exciting watching the Coronation as it was such an important event, and the television coverage seemed to last for hours.

Lorna Osbourne

Playing the Piano

Many people in our street had a piano in their front room. In most houses someone could play, even if only a little bit. Mum was really good on ours but she'd never had proper lessons. Gran had taught her as a girl, and she played for fun and just got better. She used to sing too, and would have liked to have gone on the stage, but she didn't

know how to get started. Then we kids came along so she missed out. Often on a Sunday afternoon, she'd start playing by just messing about, then we'd all end up singing the songs we'd heard on the wireless. She'd stop when she had to get tea ready. After Mum and Dad bought a television in the fifties, she stopped playing.

Ellie Roberts

Before the days of Central Heating

Our house had a coal-fired range in the living room which heated the water and was wonderful for making toast, using a long-

Dorothy Cooper (later to be Jean Ashling's Mum) dressed up for the photograph, c. 1906.

Jean Ashling aged four, ready to take a drive in 1929.

handled toasting fork. This was the warmest room in the house, especially in winter. The bedrooms were so cold that ice formed on the inside of the windows, so before we got up in the mornings, we'd pull our clothes into bed so they could warm up before we got dressed. We did have a bathroom but it had only a bath and washbasin. The toilet was outside; no soft toilet tissue in those days, it was either scratchy 'Bronco' or, more often, newspaper pages.

Lorna Osbourne

Calling for Servants

While explaining to my six-year-old niece many years ago about the working of the bell

system in our house that was still in use after 1939, she innocently enquired in a horrified tone, 'Did you keep slaves, Auntie?'

Jean Ashling

Feeding Rabbits

On the market, we often asked for outside leaves of cabbage for our rabbits. Even after the war, Mother bred rabbits for meat. Later, we used to go up The Lane (now Ladysmith Road) to pick a bagful of fresh dandelions before school for the pet rabbits. The leaves were not polluted with car exhausts like they are now.

Anne Harris, Linda Oxley and Lorna Osbourne

Listening to the Wireless

Before the advent of television, people relied on the wireless. They were kept informed of the news, and entertained by music, comedy and drama. Radio stimulates the imagination of the situations, and allows people to do other things whilst listening. As a young child in the forties, I started listening to *Dick Barton Special Agent*, and *Much Binding in The Marsh*. Later it was *The Navy Lark*, *Round the Horne*, *The Archers* and of course *The Goon Show*. I remember tuning in every week to *Hancock's Half-hour*, and then eagerly discussing the show on the bus to school the next morning. We all loved the mischief perpetrated by stars such as Sid James, Kenneth Williams, Hattie Jacques, and of course Antony Aloysius Hancock of 23 Railway Cuttings, East Cheam. Now available on cassette, these old radio programmes continue to give pleasure, though the humour may be dated.

About half past twelve each day Worker's Playtime was broadcast, coinciding with factory and home lunch times. It was a light variety show which featured many of the stars of the day. One of my favourite comedians was Arthur English, who always finished his act with the phrase 'Open the cage!'. His humour was outrageous, but never crude. In the seventies, he was the caretaker at the Grace Brothers' store in *Are You Being Served?*.

The wireless started an interest in popular orchestras and their individual styles. *Music While You Work* featured a guest orchestra or a band which would play selections of 'easy listening' songs for half an hour, from half past ten to eleven o'clock. It was simply background music, no singing.

My interest in radio has stayed with me and I still prefer it to television, despite the many good programmes that would not be successful on radio. I joined Grimsby Hospital Radio in 1978 as a hobby to help entertain patients, and I still enjoy doing that.

Brian Leonard

Come out to play!

Kids called for their friends to come out to play, not by knocking politely on the door and asking for their friend. That was the way grown-ups did it. Instead, we shouted the name of our friend through the keyhole or letterbox. The young person responded without disturbing his or her parents. Nowadays it may seem a strange process with all our modern technology of mobile phones and the internet, but in those far off days of the 50s, it was correct protocol!

Geoff Rudd

13

CHAPTER 2
Education

Chelmsford Secondary Modern School for Girls, class 1C in 1954.

Walking Free

I remember walking to school and am now quite pleased that there was no alternative, for it taught me the value of some daily exercise and, I suppose, did me good at the time. 'It'll do you good' was one of my mother's favourite sayings. It seemed to rain very heavily for days on end when I was little, and I had to wear a gabardine coat which subsequently had to be dried on a clothes airer in front of the fire during the dinner hour, if need be. My friends and I walked one mile each way, four times a day, five days a week but compared to my own parents' experiences of the same thing, it probably seemed as nothing. I remember we were able to do nearly the whole route from Manor Avenue to Welholme School via the extensive network of back passages, eight-foots and alleyways. We felt safe and were safe,

Littlecoates Junior School, class 4A in 1955. Miss Elliott was the class teacher and Mr Brocksom the Head. Sidney T. Brocksom retired in December 1956 after serving more than 45 years with Grimsby Education Authority.

being free to roam more or less where we wished as we grew older. Sadly, nearly all of these passages are now gated.

Sue Pannell

Littlecoates Games

Children at Littlecoates Junior School used the adjacent field for games. The grass was coarse, the ground uneven, and the brown patches were lethal. The cows you avoided, too.

Alan Smith

Practical Gardening

All the schools in the 1920s had their school allotments. Ours was down the bottom of

Torrington Street. We always had to walk there from school and be back at school before 4 p.m.

Eric Robinson

Failure at Wintringham

My first day at Wintringham Boys' Grammar School was a demoralizing experience. Having been an able pupil at Littlecoates Junior School, I obviously expected to be in a higher form at Wintringham. It was shattering to find that I had been placed in the lowest class.

The five years I spent at Wintringham were the longest five years of my life because I disliked it so much. I couldn't see the point of learning what I was being taught, apart from chemistry in which I came top of all four classes in the first year, with 96%.

I hated detention and on one occasion was given it for a very unjust cause (using my ruler to remove water vapour off a window). So in detention I wrote an essay saying exactly what I thought of the French teacher who had made me stay behind at the end of the working day. His face was purple with rage after he had read my honest views about him, and I thought I would be expelled. I was too frightened to tell my mother about it until we were on a train going from Hull to Hornsea. She took it very calmly, I was relieved to find.

That same French teacher was embarrassed when I also told him that he was wearing a brown and a black shoe. No wonder he never liked me! It would be good to meet him again and have a laugh about it.

Though I didn't like being in an all boys' school (and I hated communal showers) it was great fun when the girls moved into their new school across the playing fields. We boys went mad for two days until the Head, Ronald Gill, put a stop to our fun.

I hated cross-country running which we had to do, often in rain, when the football pitches were too wet to play on. We got very muddy.

In the fourth year, I was elected form captain and our class won a plaque for being the best form in the school. Unfortunately it got broken during the next year while our class was in charge of it.

One day when we arrived at school we found RHUBARB written with whitewash in huge letters across the school and most of the windows had also been painted. I thought it was funny as I disliked the school so much but today I get angry when I see graffiti.

I hated wearing my school cap and was so happy to throw it away on the day I left but then I felt guilty because my mother had had to spend money buying it – and my mother was so thrilled and proud when she learnt that I had passed the exams to get to the grammar school.

At the end of the third year I dropped history after coming bottom of the class with 29% and I gained the lowest failure grade in 'O' level English Language. I passed only two 'O' levels – maths and geography. After leaving Wintringham, I received a London University Diploma in Sociology and a Certificate of Qualification in Social Work. I was also elected as a member of The Society of Authors and most of my 23 publications are on history, so it shows that though I was under-motivated at school I have made progress since I had my happiest day at Wintringham – the day I left when I was fifteen.

John D. Beasley

Discouraged!

In our fourth year at Wintringham Boys' Grammar School, Barry and I became interested in cricket. We wanted to see how good we were and try to improve. We asked the sports master if we could use the ever-empty cricket nets. He paused, looked us up and down, and said, 'Oh no, the nets are for the team.' We lost our interest in cricket, and the nets continued to be unused.

Don Holmes

Early Days at Old Clee School

Although Old Clee Primary Junior School opened in 1951, it was not until the fol-

The Holme Hill Board Schools in Heneage Road, now used as the Teachers' Centre.

lowing year that the hall and dining rooms were completed. During the building of them, a crane lifting concrete roof sections toppled over, killing the driver. There was no playtime that afternoon. In 1953 I watched the Coronation on a television set at Huxford's, Grimsby Road, in the rain. Later the School was taken to see the Coronation film at the Ritz Cinema in Grimsby Road.

In December 1954, the school held its first Christmas Concert. The backcloth was made up of sheets of sugar paper stuck together and painted as a desert island. Some children were made up as natives using cocoa powder mixed with water. Parents later said that their baths were coated with chocolate as the children had insisted on going home still made up.

Doug Wise

First Talk Nerves

Astronomy was one of my hobbies as a teenager and the first talk I ever gave was to the Astronomical Society at Wintringham Boys' Grammar School. I spoke about the sun and can still remember how the talk began, even though I threw away the manuscript many years ago (and regret not keeping it).

How nervous I was before the talk, during it and even after the next speaker had sat down! This experience makes me very sympathetic towards nervous public speakers.

John D. Beasley

Bring back the Cane!

In junior school, the main deterrent to misbehaving was the cane. The implement itself was

The twenty-fifth anniversary of the opening of Grange Middle School brought together the three headteachers. Left to right are John Bushell, Roger Fry and Arthur Walsham.

not as rigid as the garden cane. It was more dense, supple and flexible. It certainly hurt, and made most of us 'toe the line' and think twice before we misbehaved or produced shoddy work again. We definitely did not want our friends to tell our parents that we had been caned because that would cause us to be cross-examined at home, and most likely be punished again for disgracing our family and ourselves.

At secondary school, the cane was still the ultimate deterrent, but some staff had their own methods for keeping discipline, and for maintaining their status. One history teacher, Mr H, was renowned for his command of sarcasm and his ability to belittle those who were not his best pupils. On one occasion a boy brought in a history book containing a chapter about the aspect we were studying. Mr H read a few lines to himself and made no comment. He opened the book at the front and read the inscription, 'Presented to (pupil's name), Macaulay Junior School, June 1954'. He made a bitter comment that caused the rest of the class to erupt in raucous laughter at their classmate. The boy's face fell, he took the book and sat down. He never again showed much interest in history, and failed his 'O' level badly. He would have fared better had he been caned for bringing in that book.

Mr H went on to be a headmaster elsewhere. What a sad school that must have been!

Jim Parker

Mispronunciation

Some words confused my mind as a child. I could never understand what 'mewcherlade' was, where my mother went to every Saturday afternoon at the church hall, or why the road near my Aunt's house was called Eight 'Navinew'. I often wondered what had happened to the other seven! Not seeing the spelling, and being too young to understand it, I knew little of the casual way 'ordinary' people slur their speech. Later I discovered the benefits of regularly saving in a Mutual Aid Club to pay for those extras at Christmas or to give us days out in the summer. The road near my Aunt was, of course, Hainton Avenue. She knew how it was spelt, so dropping the 'h' and other letters didn't matter to her. I accepted what I heard. However, the experience made me think words through slowly, and have since had little trouble with spelling.

Betty Fox

Disliking Games

My secondary school life was spoilt by the insistence of the school that everyone liked football and cricket. Worse still, everyone was expected to be good at them. If you had never learnt the skills, you were treated with little respect.

I much preferred a cross-country run. I could run with a friend or be alone with my thoughts, and there were no fierce competitive pressure.

John Hutton

Maths at Secondary School

Mr Clark, the maths teacher, had a pleasant but sharp sense of humour. He was asking the boys their names in his new (September) class. After Steel had answered, Mr Clark, with his not-quite-serious face said, 'Do you?' Steel, perplexed, thought it best to be positive and answered, 'Yes, sir.' Mr Clark, triumphant at catching him out, responded with mock horror, 'You don't, do you? Steal, I mean?' Recognising the game, Steel grinned and said, 'No, sir.' Maths with Mr Clark was always good fun, and we enjoyed learning.

Later I was privileged to be taught by Gerry Grainger. He was another maths teacher with a good sense of humour coupled with firm discipline. Even from being newly qualified, he was one who could explain his subject clearly and get the best out of his pupils. Looking back, I see these influences that led me to teach maths.

At my first teaching post, we had our own stock of pencils, rulers and so on, which the boys used when they came to our room. I noticed that the Head of Department's pencils were less chewed than other people's. I found out why one day when I was visiting his room. He saw a boy with a pencil in his mouth and said, not too quietly, 'I wouldn't put that pencil in your mouth, lad. (Name of scruffy older boy) had it up his nose last lesson!' The teacher told me that it always stopped them chewing his pencils!

Brian Leonard

A Frightening Experience

One day in May 1936, when I was a pupil at Nunsthorpe Junior School, everything turned a bluey-purply colour and the sky turned black. It started to thunder and lighten, then suddenly there was a loud bang. What looked like a ball of fire seemed to go through the classroom windows, fly across

Nunsthorpe Secondary School girls in 1951 or 1952. Notice the 'temporary' classroom, and houses in Second Avenue behind.

the road into the yard behind the fish shop. It seemed to spin around several times before flying off and striking the second house in Sutcliffe Avenue opposite the school. It blew out the wireless and set fire to the curtains before finishing in the back garden.

It was a most peculiar experience.

Betty Clark

Exam Interrupted by Air Raid

Wintringham Grammar School was in Eleanor Street. At the outbreak of war, the pupils were evacuated to Highfield Farm at the end of Park Avenue, the site of the present Wintringham Comprehensive School. At first we were in the farmhouse and attended either morning or afternoon, depending on the distance we lived from

school. Later huts were constructed.

My class was in one of those huts when we sat our School Certificate examinations. We had just read the questions when the air raid siren sounded, and we went into the air raid shelter. We were forbidden to talk about the questions – but we did have time to think about them!

Joyce Wilkinson

Attended Littlecoates School

What a trauma was my first day at Littlecoates School, when I was five! My mother took me inside and a teacher locked the door after my mother had left me there crying. Years later my mother told me that when I went home for dinner, I couldn't wait to get back to school to play in the sandpit.

Unfortunately I don't remember that. My only memory of my first day at school is of my mother leaving me crying in the company of teachers I didn't know and didn't want to be with. When our school was broken into, I felt very guilty as I stood outside our classroom in which the burglars had caused damage. Two boys, who were suspected of committing the burglary, were brought in a police car from Armstrong Secondary Modern School.

I was frightened of the headmaster, and lost count of the number of times I was caned when I went into one teacher's class. He used to hit me with the cane for smiling. Perhaps I saw the funny side of something when I shouldn't have done (and I still have that problem!) but he was miserable and I think he was jealous that I was happy. He used to stand girls on a desk and rub his hand up their leg. Pupils didn't think there was anything wrong, but today he would have faced disciplinary action.

When I went inside Littlecoates School for the first time after leaving over forty years earlier, I was able to tell the Head things about the school which she didn't know, like why there are shiny tiles on an outside wall. That was where the boys' outside toilets used to be.

How I remember the embarrassment when I messed my pants. I had been too embarrassed to ask my teacher for toilet paper that was kept in her cupboard – there was none in the children's toilets.

The school now has playing fields but when I was a pupil we had sport in the field next to the school and cows were kept in it. Sometimes pupils got their clothes messed up with the cow muck.

The former hall is now a library and when I visited it I saw a dolly tub, dolly stick and posser (or posher) – things which we sold in our hardware and ironmongery shop are now museum items in these days of automatic washing machines.

When I started at Littlecoates School in 1949 there were allotments on what is now part of the playground.

In the top class there was a girl who used to be punished for wetting her knickers while sitting at a double desk at the back of the classroom. I hope her enuresis would be dealt with more appropriately today.

When I was very young my mother used to take me to school in a seat at the back of her bicycle. Later I had to walk most days. When Brian Leonard became my friend I used to call at his home in Gilbey Road and then we walked together. In the winter his mother used to warm my hat, gloves and scarf before I set off on the second half of the journey.

If I had a spare penny (which wasn't very often) I used to go by tram.

On one occasion my sisters had a day off school when I didn't, so my mother bribed me to go to school by giving me tuppence.

At Littlecoates School I learnt to read, write and do basic arithmetic – and I am very grateful as they were the basis for all my future learning.

We were shown a map of the world and taught to be proud of all the countries that were in red, but we were not taught about things in English history for which we should not be proud.

John D. Beasley

Nunsthorpe Secondary School. Mr Terry's class in July 1949.

Santa Claus visited the Christmas party at Littlecoates Infants School in December 1948.

A class of Nunsthorpe Junior School in 1950. Note the corrugated roof and very loose guttering!

A Christmas party at Grange Middle School, December 1987.

CHAPTER 3
Health and Hard Times

The Grimsby and District General Hospital with front wall, and Yarborough Street on the right.

Essential Treatments

The Grimsby and District General Hospital was situated next to the Boulevard (officially, the Duke of York Gardens), a park alongside the River Freshney. Payment of one penny a week, or tuppence if a man had a family, gained you admittance to the hospital and treatment. The sum was deducted, with consent, from a man's wages. Doctor's bills were a source of worry with a visit costing from five shillings (5/-) to seven shillings and six pence (7/6). Doctor's debts were collected weekly by his own collector.

Gooseman's, the West Marsh chemist's in Corporation Road, often substituted for the doctor, and was always consulted first.

When people died, my mother was sometimes called on to wash them and 'lay them out', as it was called, but only in our neighbourhood. Then the deceased person would be placed in the coffin at home until the day of the funeral.

George Morton

Beautiful Sunday

Patients in the Grimsby and District General Hospital in Yarborough Street (the 'G and D') were entertained on a Sunday morning by a

Moving Day. Ambulances transfer patients from the old 'G & D' hospital to the new building in Scartho Road, in April 1983. On the right can just be seen the Nurses' Home, and in the centre distance is South Parade Junior School.

record request programme played on the headsets. For many years this was produced by Ken Townsend, who spent the previous Friday evening compiling and recording the show. As the programme was playing, members of the Grimsby Hospital Welfare Society toured the wards collecting requests for the following week's show. Ken always used Daniel Boone's song 'Beautiful Sunday' as the signature tune.

The motor cycle accident victims on Yarborough Ward often gave us a laugh and, being in for maybe ten or more weeks, became regular contributors.

Brian Leonard

Cider had Amazing Effect

As an Accredited Voluntary Worker for Hope UK, I have been to Slovakia four times and Kazakstan twice to do drug education work – all because of an experience in Grimsby when I was a teenager.

In a lecture for the United Kingdom Alliance in 1997, and later published as a booklet entitled 'Alcohol-Free! Prevent tragedies by reducing Britain's biggest drug problem', I stated: 'My involvement with Hope UK goes back thirty-seven years, when I left my childhood home in Grimsby at the tender age of fifteen so I could do alcohol education work at the headquarters in Westminster of what is now Hope UK... why did I want to be involved in alcohol education at such a young age? Because of my experience with cider. Though I had been brought up in a teetotal home, when I visited my aunty's home I drank cider because I thought it was non-alcoholic. Then one evening as I was walking home with my mother, after drinking some cider, I commented that I did not think I was walking as straight as I ought to be. My mother dismissed my suggestion, saying it was late. However, when I reached home I found an encyclopaedia which said that cider contains from 4 to 8 per cent of alcohol.

25

Though my parents were teetotallers, I had been ignorant of the alcoholic content of cider. I was aware that many other youngsters had not enjoyed the advantages of a teetotal upbringing, so I wanted to teach young people about alcohol. The opportunity came sooner than I expected. It was a major wrench to leave my home in Grimsby and travel 200 miles to London. Alcohol education is extremely important so I have been actively involved in this work for nearly four decades.

Alcohol education is part of the work which I do covering the whole range of legal and illegal drugs. And it all began in Grimsby!

John D. Beasley

Raising Money

Funds for the hospital were collected once a year by means of a fancily dressed and decorated horse-drawn wagon procession; entrants encouraged the spectators to place their pennies in tins or strutting nets. This carnival parade was known as the 'Biggest Ever'.

The West Marsh held its own 'Littlest Ever' because the town's 'Biggest Ever' never ventured 'over the Marsh'. We had our own flower and vegetable show on the Boulevard, a concert using local talent, with Miss Hawley's dancing class, plus dancing at night to a local band.

George Morton

'Ask Mr Sutherland'

Close to Yarborough Street on Corporation Road was Gooseman's the chemist. It was an old-fashioned shop, with many bottles of mysterious lotions on shelves behind the counter. These pharmacists provided a valuable service, giving advice and minor treatment for cuts, etc. They saved many a visit to the doctor's surgery – and a long wait. I remember Mr Sutherland, the kind and respected pharmacist at Gooseman's, lancing a large boil on the back of my hand when I was about fourteen, though it's not a story to elaborate on here!

Brian Leonard

From a Very Lucky Man

In 1945, after giving three and a half years to my King and country, I was very lucky to get a job more or less as soon as I got home, and a job which I enjoyed doing. I was in the Medical Corps which gave me a good grounding for what I enjoy doing, which is meeting and helping people. I was given the job of an ambulance driver (after I had passed all the tests) with the old Grimsby hospital. In those days, everyone paid 4d a week to keep the hospital running. It employed the staff and provided ambulances to cover the area in a twenty mile radius of the town. When I joined, there were just the three of us, but we soon became six. Each driver had an attendant, but other people used to volunteer to act as stretcher bearers.

Our ambulance had to be washed each day so we didn't go out with a dirty vehicle in the morning. In addition to daytime duties, we had to be on call every third night to take any emergencies. We still had to be ready the following morning to deal with all the clinic patients and those who were discharged.

Whilst I was at the hospital I met Mary, a lovely nurse who became my wife. After she had finished her three years' training she received the Gold Medal Award for being the most outstanding nurse in her work and exams. In those days of restrictions just after the war, she received £5 instead. She later became the operating theatre sister in charge of three theatres. As time went by, we were lucky enough to have a lovely baby girl, who I am most grateful for, as my dear wife died when my daughter was quite young. My daughter is lovely and a godsend to me after all these years, bless her.

Stanley Gilleard

Traumatic Experiences as a Child

When I was only nine, in February 1954, I heard a commotion in my house in Corporation Road. My mother came into my bedroom and told me to be very brave. Then she told me that Daddy had died and gone to Heaven to live with Jesus.

About three years later, my mother had to go into hospital. When the news was broken to me in our Lord Street home I hid behind an armchair in the front room. I feared that my mother would die and that I would have to live in the big children's home at Brighowgate. Both experiences had a profound effect on me and influenced the way I did social work in London's East End. I hated receiving children into care unless there was a plan for a better future through adoption.

John D. Beasley

Treating childhood Illnesses

The Scartho Sanatorium was later known as Springfield Hospital, gone altogether now. It

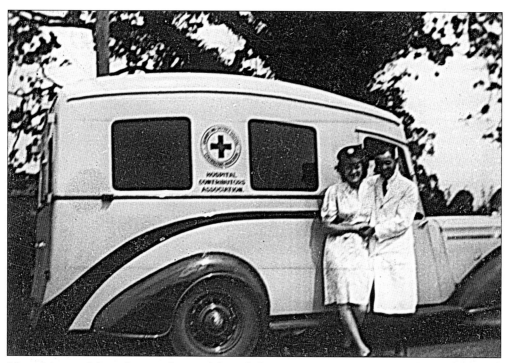

Nurse Mary and driver Stan, with one of the ambulances.

The wedding of Stanley Gilleard and Mary Chapman, on 28 August 1947, outside Flottergate Methodist Church. Standing next to the bride is her sister, Phyllis.

consisted of an isolation block for diphtheria, scarlet fever and other infectious diseases. Visitors were allowed only on Sundays, and had to converse with their children from the ground to windows up above.

The tuberculosis side of the hospital was a separate block consisting of two wards at each end of the verandah, girls in one, boys in the other, joined by the open verandah with about eight cubicles, each fitted with a single bed running at the rear. The cure for tuberculosis was named 'fresh air treatment'. Beds were left out on the verandah winter and summer. The sun would roast you in the summer, shining through the glass canopy; and the snow and ice would freeze you in winter. Often snow would drift onto the bed.

Sore throats would be painful with the iodine treatment, as would chilblains if they cracked. Parents were allowed to visit for two hours, Sundays only, and had to walk from the main road (Waltham Road) down a long lane. All sweets or eggs, etc., had to be handed in before ascending the steps. Names had to be written on the eggs, and you might get yours if you were lucky. Breakfast always consisted of porridge. Dinner was mince, potatoes and cabbage. Tea was bread and butter, and possibly the egg. Ultra violet lamps were used as sunlight treatment for the 'up' patients.

Children either perished or got well. There were no half way measures.

Looking back now, tuberculosis may have been caused by what we knew as fresh milk, which was never sterilised. Rickets was

COUGH MIXTURE.

1 oz. syrup of poppies	1 oz. horehound
1 oz. squills	1 oz. vinegar
1 oz. honey	

Mix together.   One tablespoonful 3 times a day.

CHOLERA MIXTURE.

$\frac{1}{4}$ oz. tincture rhubarb	$\frac{1}{4}$ oz. essence cayenne
$\frac{1}{4}$ oz. laudanum	$\frac{1}{4}$ oz. essence of pepperment
$\frac{1}{4}$ oz. tincture of camphor	

15 to 30 drops for a dose in cold tea or water.

Q. E. TOOTLEY.

CURE FOR RHEUMATISM.

A little powdered sulphur worn in the foot of each stocking for a few days and then replaced by fresh, is in many cases a cure for rheumatism, and it has the merit of being an inexpensive remedy, as a pennyworth would last some weeks.   Tried by a friend and found very good.

EMBROCATION.

$\frac{1}{2}$ pint vinegar	$\frac{1}{4}$ oz. spirits wine
1 oz. spirits turpentine	$\frac{1}{4}$ oz. camphor
1 egg	

Mix all together in a bottle.

Mrs. G. L. ALWARD, Waltham.

EMBROCATION.

Beat 3 eggs to a froth	$\frac{1}{2}$ pint vinegar
4 oz. spirits of turpentine	2 drachms sugar of lead

Mix the eggs, turpentine, and sugar of lead first, then add the vinegar, and shake the whole together.

Mrs. ISAAC, Waltham.

A page from The Grimsby Cookery Book (third edition) of 1910, kindly loaned by Owen Riggall. A few trusted cures are shown, recipes being supplied by local people. Three additional items added elsewhere in pencil are worth noting. Cure for wind – bicarbonate of soda; cure for 'bellyake' – soot; and cure for temper – a good hiding!

caused by malnutrition, and infectious diseases by poor sanitation. The infant mortality rate must have been very high, but large families were the norm – especially in the poorer communities.

George Morton

Preparing for New Baby

I remember Mum trotting downstairs on 2 March 1943 in her bare feet at five o'clock in the morning to put the copper on, when she knew the new baby was on the way. When the midwife came she said, 'Get up those stairs, you shouldn't be in your bare feet'. My sister was born shortly afterwards at 7 o'clock.

Anne Harris

Meeting Mentally Ill People

When I was a child, a woman dressed all in black used to walk along Corporation Road and I was scared of her because I thought she was a witch. One day, as our shop's delivery boy, I had to go to her home and I was really scared when I had to go inside to collect the money for the goods. I saw her in the back yard and I got out of the house as quickly as possible.

There was a big commotion in a West Marsh street when another woman was carried out of her house in a straitjacket, shouting and screaming, and taken to the lunatic asylum at Bracebridge. When the kindly caretaker at Flottergate Methodist Church was taken to Bracebridge, my attitude towards mentally ill people changed.

My experience of mentally ill people when

I lived in Grimsby was valuable when I became a social worker in London's East End.

John D. Beasley

When the Money Ran Out

The Grimsby Infirmary was on Scarthoe Road, opposite the Cemetery gates. The building had previously been the Grimsby Workhouse. When people became destitute, with no wife or husband to support them, the workhouse was the last hope. In exchange for a bed and some food, they were made to do any work assigned to them. A lot of people wound up there. In those days not many people owned a house and the constant fear for a lot of poor families was that the children would be taken away and the parents would end up in the workhouse. It was only a short journey across the road to a pauper's grave.

Of the children, boys usually ended up in a Naval school and the girls were placed 'in service', that is, a lackey in some well-to-do home.

George Morton

Growing up after the First World War

Beginnings

I was born in a very small house, situated down a street passage. For reasons unknown to me, four or five other such homes were erected, so that the houses that made up the streets were in the front of the ones where my mother and her brood were living. All the streets were erected on the same plans.

At this time, as I learnt as age crept on me, there were my three younger brothers with mother. Father was then somewhere in France with the army in the First World War.

I made my debut on 30 August 1915, there already being Richard, Charlie and George. I was a small weakling, not expected to be with the family much longer – so the doctor told my mother at that time, but I managed to keep going.

Earliest Memories

My first memory is of being lifted on my eldest brother's shoulder, and being amongst the crowds of people waiting along Freeman Street, as far as the eye could see. They were all hoping to catch sight of the husbands, sons, uncles or lovers among the soldiers who were marching through the town. The year did not concern me much then, and I don't know to this day what year it was. I do remember being with brother Dick at the corner of Garibaldi Street near Reinick's Soft Drinks Saloon. There, a penny bought a glass of dandelion and burdock, or other soft drink, and we would sit down at the tables inside. I was of a tender age, so I think this must have been in 1919 or 1920.

Father comes Home

My next memory is of an event that was to have a big impact on the whole family for many years to come. When my father came home, another man came to escort him. It turned out that my father had been shot in the head, and the bullet had blinded him. As a result, he was admitted to a St. Dunstan's Home for service men and women blinded in the Great War. The escorting man became a close friend to both my mother, father and to us boys in the years that followed.

So many young men went to war from the year 1914, leaving behind girlfriends and young newly-wed brides, in their thousands. Many soon found themselves pregnant. The mere fact that these women were to become mothers while their husbands or lovers were absent was accepted as a fact of life. No one was really amazed or thought of scandal, but made the best of what was to be a real struggle for families.

St Dunstan's Gives Help

Father was soon fully trained by St Dunstan's in the skills of Boot and Shoe Maker and Repairer. Wooden clogs were

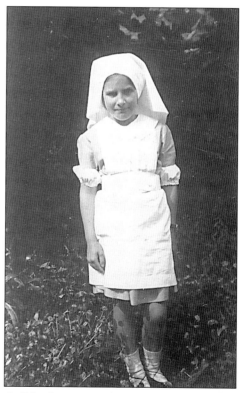

Call for the nurse! – Jean Ashling ready to help her dad.

worn by many men and women in the fishing industry, and father became a leading clog maker in the town.

St Dunstan's arranged for our family to move to a two-bedroomed house, behind and above a shop in Nelson Street – number 47. It was only a few doors away from the Corporation Arms pub on the corner of Nelson Street and Freeman Street. Opposite was the Black Bull pub, and there was The Railway pub at the corner of Railway Street and Nelson Street. Both these public houses have been gone a long time now.

Settling Down

Within a year or two, my father had made a very good name for himself and trade was good. He did boot and shoe repairs for footwear shops in town, and fishermen's clogs were always being made or repaired.

Many nights he would sit in the kitchen in front of the fire finishing some footwear, be it a pair of boots, shoes or clogs, even after we boys had gone to bed.

The amazing thing about our family was how well we coped with a blind father in the house. We were NOT allowed in his shop because everything was put where he wanted, so that by touch he was always able to put his hands on whatever he wanted. Mother would help him by writing out the name tags for the customers' repairs, but he handled the money and knew the coins by the touch of his fingers. He was supplied with a Braille watch, and later a Braille typewriter.

We lads Helped

During these years, one of the jobs delegated to us boys was to collect clogs from Fish Houses and the docks for repair, then to return the repaired clogs to the places where they had come from. We had an old pram to carry the footwear, but later we made our own barrows to suit our size. We usually got a penny or two for our long and tiring work. We were well pleased too, and so was mother, when we brought some fish straight off the docks or smoked fish from the Fish Houses.

These fish curing houses were mostly in the Victor Street area, from Cleethorpe Road right down to Welholme Road, with some on the docks and others in the Riby Street area.

In those days every public house had a 'Bottle and Jug' room, where people could bring their own jug, usually with a lace cloth over the top, and have it filled. Wives sent their children to bring back the ale for themselves or for their husbands. I made this journey many times when I was quite young.

I can also recall that the landlady of the 'Black Bull' annually organised a collection to pay for all the kiddies of the street to have a day out at Cleethorpes with their mothers. This outing was paid for by the pennies put into a large bottle, and raffles or whatever means she could devise.

My family's Background

My mother was born within the sound of 'Bow Bells' in London, thereby being a true Cockney. She would often sit down and tell us boys of her younger days. She had two sisters. My Auntie May married an American soldier and joined her husband in the United States. I met her only once when I was younger. The other sister, my Auntie Flo, went into service somewhere in Kent. My mother herself entered service at twelve years of age in London at a lawyer's house, then moved to service with a family butcher living in Bedford.

I don't know where or when she met my father, but it must have been before the First World War. They were married at Old Clee Church.

Mother's Present

When my parents were married, Father was a soldier with the Lincolnshire Yeomanry. In 1902 his mother had told him she had a birthday present for him. She took him to the Army Recruitment Office and enlisted him as a boy soldier. Two years later in 1904 he transferred to the Lincolnshire Regiment.

A Strict Upbringing

With the combination of an ex-soldier for a father, and a mother who had entered service in her early years, we children were always taught right from wrong. Each one of us was never allowed to answer back, or swear, and was each given a weekly chore in the house – cleaning and pumice-stoning two doorsteps, cleaning the cutlery, black-leading the fireplaces, scrubbing the wooden toilet seat, swilling the backyard, and generally doing jobs in the house – to mother's approval. We did the job more than once if it was not done properly. We were always told to be polite, not only at home. 'Never expect anything then you will not be disappointed', I recall my father always telling us boys. 'Be as honest as you can afford, too, and use your brains'. They were both loving, but strict, without being bullies to us.

At the age of five I was taken by Mother to Strand Street School. It was then that I

W. K. GRESSWELL, House and Estate Agent,

ADDITIONAL RECIPES.

Cough Mixture

2ᵈ peppermint
2ᵈ oil of Aniseed
2ᵈ Laudanum
1 oz Spanish Juice
1 lb dark treacle
1 pt water
1 wineglass vinegar

Crush spanish juice & put into pan with treacle, water & vinegar until quite dissolved
When cold add other ingredients put into a wine bottle & shake well   39, Freeman Street, GRIMSBY.
1 or 2 tablespoonsfull 3 times a day

A cure for a cough added to the Grimsby Cookery Book of 1910, by Mrs Riggall.

felt I was beginning to grow up. There was so much to learn every day; it was a great adventure.

Some Sad Sights

It was sad to see on the street corners small gatherings of old soldiers who had survived the war, many having suffered gas attacks, having lost arms or legs, or who had become deaf from cannon fire, or even lost their sight as did my father. These small groups of heroes with highly polished medals, heads held high, stood in their often tattered clothes or remains of wartime uniforms. Some even had to resort to busking in the streets, outside pubs and picture houses, singing together with a squeeze box or old mouth organ. They often carried placards around their neck proclaiming 'Gassed in France', or 'Ex-

Ambulance drivers and a clerk posing on the steps of the Grimsby and District Hospital in South Parade, c.1946. Note the bicycle leaning against the wall (right), which would still be there at leaving time.

Serviceman – crippled – no work – no money – Please spare a penny or two'. It was an everyday normal sight. I knew an old soldier who had lost both legs. He got about on a small home-made trolley with four small wheels, a few inches above ground level. He used both arms to propel himself on the trolley. I often spoke to this man in the streets.

Slowly though, day by day, the people were getting the feeling that at last the worst was being put behind them. Families were more united, and gone were the days of real poverty and misery.

Eric Robinson

CHAPTER 4
Transport

Artist's drawing of Central Market, the terminus of bus routes 5 and 7. Note (extreme right) the step bridge over the railway to Newmarket Street.

The Eye Never Lies!

Where in Grimsby is GILEBY Road? For years many local buses displayed this place on their destination blinds, and few people noticed the mistake. We all saw what we expected to see – GILBEY Road. Who transposed the letters E and B? The person ordering the destination blinds, or someone at the suppliers? We shall never know... unless this book prompts someone to provide the answer.

Chris Stephens

Light Rail

The modern Light Rail systems of Sheffield, Manchester and London Docklands are comfortable and environmentally friendly. But in 1912 we had our own similar system – the Grimsby Immingham Electric Light Railway. Installed and operated by the Great Central Railway (later the L.N.E.R.), it carried thousands of workers between the two towns until it became 'unfashionable' in the early 1960s, and was replaced by diesel buses, doubling the distance and travelling time. Now that 'Light Rail' is in fashion again, will

Daimler MEE 350 (fleet number 110) turning into the Victoria Street depot, soon after arriving new in 1959. Redevelopment opposite is not yet complete.

we see a modern version of the Grimsby to Immingham tramway system?

Geoff Rudd

Buses of the 1950s

Central Market was the terminus for buses to the West Marsh. The number 5 went to the far end of Gilbey Road, and the number 7 travelled via Corporation Road, Boulevard Avenue, some side streets into Lord Street, Alexander Road, and back to Central Market. The number 7 returned along the same route in reverse. To be ready for the return journey, the buses would circle the clock tower, before pulling up at the bus shelter.

Both routes used the double deck AEC Regent mark I, with centre entrance bodies, a design rarely seen in other towns. As passengers decreased, they were replaced by the single deck AEC Regals, fleet numbers 64 to 67 and 69 (JV 8275-8 and 8280). We teenage bus-spotters of the late 1950s were intrigued by the absence of vehicle 68. I found out later that its body was destroyed in 1943, rebuilt, and 68 was withdrawn, apparently with a petrol engine, in 1955.

Regals were also used on route number 2, Old Market Place to Drew Avenue, because of the low bridges carrying the railway over Doughty Road. The occasional double decker bus did use this street, but became an 'instant' single decker in the process!

Ray Woods

AEC Regal and driver at the Drew Avenue terminus of the 2X route from Old Market Place. Route 2X travelled via Hainton Avenue instead of along Farebrother Street.

One of the first batch of AEC Reliance single deck buses, in Old Market Place on the first day of the new service 45 to Immingham.

Bus Destroyed

The day following the air raid of 12-13 June 1943, a fellow messenger told me that a bus passenger had found a butterfly bomb under a rear seat of the upper deck of bus number 44. The bus was driven out to Waltham very slowly with a police escort. There the bomb was detonated. I saw number 44 the following day with extensive damage to its rear. A week or so later I saw 44 back in service, having had its body replaced with that from number 62 (built 1937). When 44 was withdrawn in 1950, the 1937 body was transferred to number 53.

Norman Drewry

New Buses Admired

After years of 'make do and mend' – giving older vehicles new bodies – Grimsby Corporation Transport invested in some modern single deck buses in 1956. Of a new revolutionary design, these six AEC Reliance vehicles (HEE 820 – 825) caused many heads to turn. They had underfloor engines, separate entrances and exits with doors controlled by the driver, and were very light and fresh inside.

Derek Hill

An Exciting Journey

Kids loved going to Cleethorpes from Old Market Place by 'the other way' – the number 6 route via Weelsby Road. If you were lucky, you didn't travel on a maroon and cream bus (Grimsby's), but a pale blue and grey one (Cleethorpes'), which sounded different too. The journey seemed longer, it may have cost more, but there were pretty views,

A bus arriving in the Bull Ring at the Cromwell Florist stop. It terminated in Town Hall Street before returning to Waltham. Set back behind the tree was Church House.

The last tram from Immingham to Grimsby arriving at Cleveland Bridge with invited guests on 1 July 1961.

unfamiliar streets, a deep subway, AND trees along the roadside. We had to sit upstairs so we could hear the overhanging trees hit the tops of the buses – that was exciting!

Maureen Thompson

Trains at Littlefield Lane

My early memories of Grimsby are of visiting my Grandma and Granddad for our summer holiday in the 1950s. As children we used to play on the spare ground next to the railway line in Littlefield Lane. We never dreamed of going over the railings or trespassing onto the line. We just liked to play there on the grass.

We did look forward to the steam trains coming along. I even got to know one or two engines. 'That's a Standard', or 'It's a Namer'

was shouted out with great excitement. We used to stand in awe, watching the engine waiting at the signal. The level crossing gates would open, the signal would go up and the train chuffed slowly forward, the black smoke and grey steam belching from its chimney.

We used to watch the signalman moving from side to side in his box high above the line. We could not see what he was doing – just that he was moving something about!

Three boys used to come to train spot and we became friends with them. They told us about the engines and where they had come from. Some were from Sheffield packed with holiday makers on their annual trip to Cleethorpes. One day when I came back to Grimsby, I saw one of these young men on Grimsby Town Station. Yes, he had become an employee of British Railways!

When I pass over Littlefield Lane crossing now as an adult, I can still see in my mind's

The end of an era, as the tower wagon (EE 8128) dismantles the overhead power cables of the trolley system, outside Timothy Whites' chemist's shop in Victoria Street.

The forlorn sight of three redundant trolley buses in Hill's scrapyard off Armstrong Street in 1960.

eye a big black engine waiting for the gates to open.

Sandra Leonard

Electric Buses Replace Trams

Grimsby's electric trams ran from Cleethorpes, through Old Market Place, over Deansgate Bridge, along Bargate, left into Welholme Road, and ended by the park gates at Ainslie Street corner. What a shame the replacement trolley bus route was stopped at the Old Market. We can only speculate what might have been the eventual destination had the route continued along Bargate. Perhaps there could have been a circular route joining with the Freeman Street-Hainton Avenue route, via Welholme Road or even Weelsby Road. We might have seen trolley buses reach Bradley Cross Roads or even Scartho. Who knows?

Barry Hall

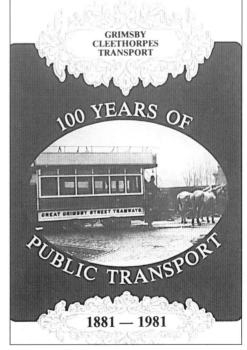

GRIMSBY CLEETHORPES TRANSPORT

100 YEARS OF

GREAT GRIMSBY STREET TRAMWAYS

PUBLIC TRANSPORT

1881 — 1981

The cover of the Grimsby Cleethorpes Transport Centenary booklet, showing a horse tram at Park Street depot on the first day of operation, 4 June 1881.

Trolley bus No. 164 speeding along the curve at Lock Hill, after the old buildings had been demolished, the tight corner had been removed and the trolley bus wires realigned. A major roundabout now occupies this site, though the new building (right) remains.

Bus 37 (a Guy Arab II with utility body) was bought second-hand from Sunderland in 1957. The mechanic is Tim Coleman, who was often responsible for putting the vehicles through their annual inspection, before MOT tests were introduced for cars.

Diesel Replaces Electric

Trolley buses were used in many towns until electricity could no longer compete with cheap imported oil. Quiet, efficient, low maintenance electric buses accelerated quickly between frequent stops. Then, the electricity industry was nationalised, causing prices to rise, and some towns scrapped their trolleys in favour of the mass produced diesel bus. Others hung on to their electric buses, but new vehicles were too expensive as manufacturers increased vehicle costs to off set lower production. Repairing the overhead equipment became costly, and extending routes to distant new housing estates was out of the question. Grimsby's number ten route went first, and the whole system closed in June 1960. Many enthusiasts came to the town to ride on the last vehicles.

Barry Hall

4472 The Flying Scotsman visited Grimsby on several occasions after being bought from British Railways by Alan Pegler. Here it passes the town station on the avoiding lines on a wet and windy day in 1968. Note the cooling towers in the background.

Nine-year-old Drives Bus

A dad went to see his son's teacher at the beginning of the school year in September. The dad said, 'I don't want you telling my lad off, or you'll have me to deal with.' The child was always misbehaving and rude, but what else could you expect with his father's consent and support?

One day a couple of months later the boy, a diminutive nine-year-old, was absent from school. While walking down Victoria Street, he passed the bus depot. The thought must have struck him, 'Why don't I go for a ride in this bus parked here at the side of the road. Dad would say it's okay.' So

he did. He stood at the controls, started the engine, and drove the double-decker along the main road to Cleethorpes. There was no Lock Hill roundabout then, and all the traffic lights were green.

All was well until he tried to go around Isaac's Hill roundabout. Even with power assisted steering, he could not turn the wheel fast enough. The bus embedded itself in the front room of a house on the downhill side of the road. The boy was not hurt and, thankfully, no innocent person was either. His teacher never saw him again.

It emerged later that he had previously stolen a milk float for 'fun'. Had anyone explained to him that children should not steal vehicles? The bus incident made head-lines in the *Grimsby Evening Telegraph* that night.

As told by the child's teacher

Opened too Late

The Cleethorpe Road flyover was opened in 1968, to ease the congestion when frequent, long fish trains caused ever increasing block-ages at the level crossing. During the building of the bridge, fish movement was transferred to road. About the same time, the day tripper trains from the Midlands ceased as more people travelled by car. The flyover is virtually unnecessary nowadays, but demo-lition would be too expensive.

Derek Hill

By Steam Train to London

When I was six, as a treat my mother took me to London for a day by steam train. We went to Buckingham Palace, to the zoo, into Selfridges and on the Underground. When we arrived home, my Dad opened the back door and the first thing I said was: 'Dad, I got some fourers'. Despite all the exciting things I had seen in London, the highlight of the day was seeing trains beginning with the number 4 instead of 6, which is all I ever saw when my sister took me train spotting at Grimsby Town Station.

When I was fifteen I left my home in Grimsby to work in London. A steam train took me to London via Louth on 3 October 1960. Later, under the Beeching axe (which was one of the biggest mistakes of the twen-tieth century), the line was closed – thus preventing me from returning to live in Grimsby, I sometimes jokingly say.

John D. Beasley

New Design Failed

In 1932, Grimsby Corporation Transport pur-chased one of only twenty-three double deck buses built to a new revolutionary design. The AEC Q type was twenty-five years ahead of its time. It had a side-mounted engine (under the central stairs) and looked so much like the cen-tral entrance trolley buses that many people thought it had been converted from one of them. When new, each bus cost £1,225. 326 single decker buses with the same chassis design were built, mainly for London Transport.

Its body style did indeed resemble the trol-ley buses, both being designed and built by the same company, Charles Roe & Co. of Leeds. However, the Q type, Grimsby fleet number 48, was shorter, ran on two axles not three, and allowed passengers to sit at the side of the dri-ving position, which was not possible on the trolley buses. Sadly, sales did not meet expec-tations. It may have been that the engine was considered too inaccessible for the mechanics of the time. London Transport put its orders with AEC, and it ordered hundreds of vehicles of the STL type, not the Q. Perhaps there was-n't the factory space, but whatever the reason, many of the Q type's features were not seen again until the late 1950s.

Derek Hill

Travelling by Tram

Corporation Road was served by a number 5 corporation bus running between New

One of the larger Grimsby-Immingham trams in LNER livery on its way to Grimsby.

Market Square and Cleveland Street, fare one penny (1d). It was also served by the Immingham trams. Owned by the LNER and running on basically single track, the trams were able to pass each other by means of a number of loop lines on both street and country sections. Where the track ran along the street, the rail was set into the roadway so other vehicles could use the roads. The signals were exchanged by the driver of the oncoming tram to the trams waiting in the loop, by raising the number of fingers to indicate the number of following trams. It was a bit scary in fog, but I never knew of any accidents, and I rode them between 1939 and 1961. Every part of them vibrated or moved whilst they were in motion because all the upper structure was slotted in, even the windows. The wooden seats were slotted into the frame, and by moving the backrest the seat could face either way. Four people could play solo whist (the game of engine crews) whilst they were travelling. Plate layers played rummy, with a coat laid over their knees as a table.

George Morton

Unusual Buses visit Grimsby

Saturday 28 June 1958 was a special day for Grimsby. The Queen was visiting the town. I planned to stand in Victoria Street to watch the procession.

As I reached Boulevard Avenue/ Corporation Road corner, the first green bus pulled up to the 'halt' sign on Boulevard Avenue. It turned into Corporation Road, and another green bus pulled up. There were ten altogether, all marked 'Lincoln City Transport'. They had been loaned to

45

One of the six-wheel trolley buses in Hainton Avenue at the Weelsby Road terminus of the number 10 route to Riby Square. Notice the well-clipped trees.

The experimental AEC 'Q' type double decker, seen on the bomb site where the police station was later built.

Grimsby trolley bus no.19 waits for 'time' at the Hainton Avenue terminus on 28 August 1958. The houses on the far left are in Weelsby Road at the top of the subway.

Grimsby to assist in moving hundreds of schoolchildren to the King George V Playing Field ready for the Queen's visit. They must have travelled along Littlecoates and Yarborough Roads to avoid the town centre.

Chris Stephens

Number 13 was Missing

I remember seeing many centre door trolley buses on Grimsby's streets (registration numbers JV5001 to JV5010). They were usually deployed on the number ten route from Riby Square to Weelsby Road. Their numbers began at 8 and finished with 18, but there were only ten of them – number 13 was missing. Its registration number would have been JV 5006. However, that registration was allocated to number 18. So why was this strange order? The reason given was that Grimsby's fishermen were very superstitious and would not have ridden on a vehicle carrying 13, such a notoriously unlucky number!

Ray Woods

Afternoon traffic in Old Market Place, busy for a grey Sunday in 1954. The tower of the Corn Exchange stands firm, a symbol of security linking Grimsby's past with its present, but sadly not its future. In a few years, all would be changed.

CHAPTER 5
Shops and Businesses

Where the Corn Exchange once stood in Old Market Place, here used to park a wide variety of cars. The Black Swan (Mucky Duck!) is seen in the distance, and notice the range of building styles.

Shopping in Nunsthorpe

Until I married, I was brought up in Sutcliffe Avenue near Second Avenue where I was born. I remember the wide variety of local shops in Second Avenue where almost anything could be bought.

On one side was Whiting's the grocer's, Wilkinson's the newsagent's and sweet shop, Lambert's the barber's (as they were known

Fred Beasley standing in the doorway of his ironmongery and hardware shop. Such was the need for these businesses, Corporation Road boasted two hardware shops.

in those days) and Mr Pearson the cobbler, who lived above his shop. The cobbler's shop had one doorway but was divided into two inside; the other part was taken over by Jim Schofield as a cycle repair shop. Next to the cobbler's was rough open land on which there was a brick or concrete high water reservoir. On the corner of Kingsley Grove was the local branch of the Co-operative Society, the largest shop which sold mainly groceries.

On the other side was Ye Olde Chippe Shop run by Mr Rayton, the Supply Stores (another grocer's) run by Mr Ellerby, Williamson's the butcher's, Bradbury's the greengrocer's, then more waste ground. On the waste ground near the cobbler's was a raised bit which I believe to have been his air-raid shelter. Along with some of my friends we used to play on this with our home-made trolleys. Many times he or his wife came out and told us to play somewhere else. So we did, otherwise we would have been in trouble with our parents because he knew us all.

During the 1950s, the Co-operative Society built a general shop selling clothes and electrical goods on this land. The waste land on the other side, which we also played on, was later built on by the Trustee Savings Bank, with a wine and spirits shop next door. I remember going to the Supply Stores for sugar which was weighed and bagged for us, also butter or margarine which was cut, weighed and wrapped in what quantity we wanted. I think that we could take an empty tin and have it filled with treacle.

David Bradley

Unfair Competition

I remember accompanying my mother to Mary Cribb's greengrocer's and florist's shop opposite Flottergate Church. Mary (who died in March 2001) was in tears because Burgon's, next door to the Ship Hotel, had placed a bucket of flowers for sale outside their shop. 'My livelihood will go if others sell things I have always sold', she complained. I wonder, was this the beginning of the supermarket era?

Jean Ashling

Cattle Markets and Abattoirs

Having a large concentration of population in a predominantly rural area, Grimsby was a natural centre for the farming communities round about. This was especially true for livestock keepers. Grimsby always had thriving cattle markets and slaughter houses. Brighowgate bus station is where Grimsby's cattle market stood. Situated at the side of the railway, it received and despatched hundreds of animals by train whenever the market was held. A few pens remained at the side of the track into the 1980s. Many animals arrived by road, later in lorries, but in the early days they were herded along the streets. When this market closed, the business transferred to a site between Cromwell Road and the railway, next to what is now Boulevard Avenue subway. All livestock movements were then by lorry. It too closed in due course.

The modern slaughterhouse was also on Cromwell Road, nearer to the Willows Estate. However, there had been a small one on Holles Street before the site was redeveloped for the new Asda superstore. I remember cycling past one Saturday morning in 1957, when a lorry load of sheep arrived. I stopped to watch, with a dozen other people, while the sheep were unloaded and moved into the building. There was a lot of forlorn bleating, and a sickening smell in the air. I think the animals realised in their limited way what was about to happen.

Ernest Wilson

Sikh Men came into Shop

When I was a child, Sikh men came into our shop trying to persuade my parents to buy things. They looked so tall with their tur-

Elsie Beasley ready to serve customers with paraffin, a dolly tub or some nails, in the family's shop at 127 Corporation Road.

Lee's newsagent's in Grimsby's Bull Ring was typical of the quaint shops which gave this area its much missed character. St James' Church tower stands above the roof line. Butchery Lane leads off to the left.

ping centre was Corporation Road, where there were greengrocers, butchers, bakers, ironmongers, haberdashers, clothing stores, a chemist and a pet shop. My favourite was Howden's the butchers, near to Yarborough Street corner. Their 'Savoury Ducks' (minced beef and flavourings) were so tasty, the treat of the week!

Ray Woods

Working at Old Clee Farm

Vegetables

In winter, swedes and a large dry cereal, like cornflakes, were fed to cattle. We had a machine that was turned by hand, producing swede chips, to make them small enough for the cattle to eat. Swedes and kale were taken up by hand in winter, by the two full-time farmhands. When snow covered the fields, it was a horrible job. They always went home for meals.

To keep potatoes over winter, they were stored in a pile. They were covered by a thick soil layer to keep out the frost. We dug a shallow trench around the pile to drain the water away and keep the crop dry.

bans. I was frightened of them. They were the only people born abroad that I had met until I was fifteen and moved to London, where I have had the enriching and mind-broadening experience of meeting people from around the world.

John D. Beasley

Shopping down Corporation Road

Like many other towns, Grimsby lost hundreds of small family businesses and shopkeepers with the advent of the supermarket. One shop-

Stacks and Ruts

Harvesting sometimes went into October. It would be almost dark when the last load was brought in. The men working in the fields would quench their thirst with cold tea without milk. The bottles were put in a ditch to keep them cold.

All corn was kept in a stack. At threshing time, a steam engine powered a drum,

a machine that separated grain from the stalks and husks, etc. An elevator lifted the straw onto the stack. That was quite exciting for us children to watch. We kids wanted to play on the hay and corn stacks. We were told to keep off because we would make them leak if the thatch was damaged.

The operation was surrounded by wire netting to stop rats escaping out of the stacks. A couple of wire-haired terrier dogs were very efficient at killing the rats. The dogs were the pets of the farmhands. We youngsters would also chase the rats with sticks to kill them.

Animals

There was always a competition to see who could un-tether the goat to bring it in at night. You were seen as 'tough' if you could handle it. We held on to its rope, but it would run so fast, making us scrape our knuckles on the corners of the buildings or fall flat on the ground. It was the only goat on the farm, so I don't know why they kept it.

I used to round up the cows with the aid of a small dog, Genie. She was a 'Heinz 57', a bit of a sheepdog, and a lovely old thing. Once a cow got stuck in a ditch, and sank into the soft mud. Her mooing was a pitiful sound to hear. It took four men with ropes to pull her out.

We watched kids use the mounting stone near the barn to get up onto a horse. An old tradition was to spit and make a wish. Sometimes we would hide in the barn and make weird noises to try to frighten them.

David Edwards

Evington's shop in the Bull Ring. Note the wall of the sunken toilets on the right, and the gathering of pigeons on the shop roof!

Shopping in Brighowgate

Some of my earliest memories are of shopping with my mother in the 1950s. We took our weekly order to Peart's in Brighowgate, where Philip Duguid, who later became a family friend, weighed up sugar, tea, tub butter, etc. while we waited. Everything was put in a big brown box for a delivery boy to bring round on his bike later that day, and the cost of each item was written in a book alongside the item. I found this shopping extremely boring and my mother used to bribe me to be more patient with the promise of a few sweets from Noble's next door when we had finished.

Sue Pannell

53

Freeman Street market square

West Marsh Industries

The West Marsh area of Grimsby (Little
Russia) was enclosed by the Alexandra
Docks to the east, the Humber to the north,
and the River Freshney (The Haven) to the
south. The industry consisted mainly of
wood yards, sawmills, and Dixon's Paper
Mill. The imports of wood or pulp to serve
these enterprises came principally from
Scandinavia and Russia, which resulted in a
huge complex of railway sidings to the rear
of these industries, now vanished.

George Morton

Shopping in the East Marsh

We went to Mrs Overan to get the bread. It
was nice crusty bread and we used to chew
the corners as we carried it home. It looked
as if mice had been at it.

There was a greengrocer's on the corner of
Durban Road. Landles, a general store, was
on the corner of Durban Road and Ladysmith

Road, and it's still run by the same family.

Across the road was a baker's. My brother
Michael delivered hot rolls in the morning.
We always used to go to Dewhurst the
butcher's on Freeman Street. They were
very famous.

On Saturdays we went to Freeman Street
market with Mum. I loved to watch the men
selling pots. They would hold up a whole tea
set and not drop it or break any of it. If you
went to the fruit and veg stalls at the end of
the day, they would sell some of the produce
cheaper. It was a treat for us to go into
Reinecke's, opposite the Regal cinema, to
have a drink. In winter I'd have hot black-
currant and in summer I'd have orange. I can
still feel the steamy atmosphere of that place.

*Anne Harris, Linda Oxley
and Lorna Osbourne*

Ice Cream Heaven

We went down an alley (an eight-foot) off
Sixhills Street from the Ladysmith Road end

to Ada's, well-known ice cream makers. There was a wooden counter, and the ice cream was made at the back. We were often sent to buy a basin full, and had to dash home before it melted. This was around 1950.

Anne Harris

Corporation Road in the '50s

As a child I was known as Boffulls (and I still tell people that's my nickname) but Roger Markham who invented it didn't know why. Roger lived on Corporation Road and a pig was kept in the alley which led to his house.

In the same block was St Paul's Church and opposite was the bomb site where we had a big bonfire on 5 November. My Dad used to provide the paraffin for lighting it. For many years I had a scar on my forehead where part of a brick hit me after a banger went off. If it had been a little lower I would have been blinded in one eye.

On the other side of the road, close to the Rex cinema, was a petshop whose owner used to eat dog biscuits saying that if they were good enough for dogs they were good enough for him.

All our food shopping was done within a hundred yards of our home. We saved the paper bags for putting screws and nails in when customers came to our hardware and ironmongery shop. We sold putty loose from a metal drum. We wrapped it in the waxed paper that surrounded sliced bread. In the 1940s and '50s we reused things to save money. Now I recycle and reuse 'rubbish' to help preserve the planet's resources.

In my workshop in Peckham, where I enjoy woodwork as a hobby, I have a magnet which came from our shop. They cost 2/6

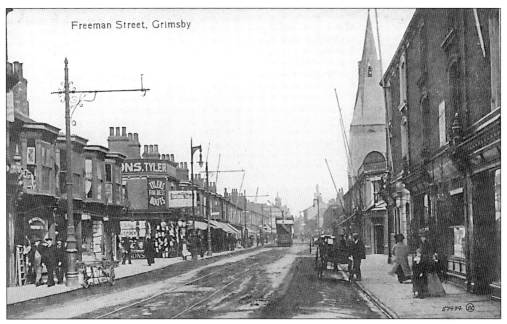

Freeman Street in the days when trams and carts were the only danger to pedestrians. The spire belongs to St Andrew's Church.

The Robinsons kept this shop in Albert Street, off Freeman Street. The baby in the chair, Lilian, was born on 16 October 1896, and became organist at St Andrew's Church before she joined the Anglican Order of St Wilfred's in Exeter, later becoming Reverend Mother. Mr Robinson moved to premises at 65 Pasture Street and remained in business there into his eighties. The Robinson's grandson, Norman Drewry, loaned several of the transport photographs in chapter 4.

which I did not have in about 1948, so I stole it from our shop. When my Dad saw me playing with it he asked if I had paid for it and I said 'Yes'. When I am giving children's talks in churches I sometimes show the magnet and confess that I stole it from my Dad and lied to him. I then urge the children not to be naughty as I was but to follow the example of Jesus who was an honest person.

John D. Beasley

Free Rides

Mr Stubbs owned a greengrocer's shop on the corner of Columbia Road and Weelsby Street. He had a horse and cart for his deliveries, he used to let us ride on it.

*Anne Harris, Linda Oxley
and Lorna Osbourne*

Errand Boy

My after-school job as a teenager was to deliver for Colebrook's, the pet food shop on Flottergate. I went each evening after school for an hour, and every Saturday from 9.30 to 12.30. The repair and maintenance of the bike was part of the job. It was a 'carrier' bike, with a small front wheel, over which was a frame to hold a large metal container. A pair of legs dropped down to enable the bike to stand. The gearing was very low, so speed was out of the question, and with a full container, peddling was hard work. In wet weather a cover fitted over the front to keep the deliveries dry. The rider provided his own protection!

My pay was twelve and six a week (12/6). Today's lads would not do it.

Peter Hewitt

Charging the Radio Battery

It took two of us to take the radio battery to be charged. Michael and I would carry it between us to where there was a garage type place in Durban Road and bring another one back, leaving the old one to be charged. (Before the use of transistors, and before mains radios became widely available, radios were powered by two batteries. A high tension – voltage – battery operated the valves, and a low voltage one heated the valves so they would work properly.)

Anne Harris

A Special Railway Service

In the 1940s I was a schoolboy, having been born in 1935. My dad was employed by the local railway (London North Eastern Railway) but worked as a railwayman (with trains) for only the final few years of his life.

If that sounds strange, it is because he was

The staff of Colebrook's pet supplies shop pausing for a photograph in 1959. The side street to the left was Red Hill.

Sidney and Ethel Craggs on their wedding day. Sid worked at the railway bakery which supplied many local stations with bread and pastries.

employed as a van driver for the Royal Dock Bakery in Grimsby. The bakehouse from which he operated was behind the Royal Dock Chambers. To the right, as you looked at the Chambers, was a side street which led to the Union Dock and the Royal Dock. Across this street was the Royal Hotel. The Cleethorpe Road flyover now occupies the site of these buildings.

The Royal Dock Chambers housed such firms as Bannister's, the coal and export merchant's. Incidentally, my mother worked as housekeeper for Bannister's managing director and his wife, Mr and Mrs Rudolph David.

As a schoolboy, and an only child with both parents working, during the school hol-idays it fell to me to go to work with one or other of my parents. Certainly the most adventurous 'outing' was going to work with Dad. There were two reasons for this: I rode in his van (we didn't have a car) and I travelled with him as far afield as Mablethorpe and Skegness, as well as doing all the local runs. Also, I was allowed into the bakery to watch the staff making the bread, cakes, pork pies and sausage rolls – and was often permitted to sample them!

It would not be allowed today but it was exciting to watch the huge oven doors being opened and the food being fed in, or taken out, and to see the huge gas-fed flames doing their job in the cooking process. It was nothing short of miraculous to see the change in the items after cooking and to see the trays of food set out for Dad to pack into his van and deliver.

Dad's job was to deliver to the various refreshment rooms on the railway stations in the Lincolnshire area and to at least two refreshment rooms on the Fish Docks in Grimsby.

The first time I went with him on the Fish Docks, he told me to stay in the van while he made the delivery because it was a dangerous place for a youngster to be. The floors were very slippery with water and fish slime. The lumpers were used to it and knew just how to walk in their heavy clogs, but it was hard to keep your feet if you weren't used to it.

It was not long before I felt that I was clever enough to negotiate the distance between the van and the canteen. After suffering much cajoling, Dad let me carry some small trays 'as long as you keep close to me'. The lumpers were a jolly crowd and they cheered me on and gave me confidence – but too much. When I fell, covering my clothes with slime and scattering cakes all over the place, a great cheer went up and lots of men

The Royal Hotel, next to Cleethorpe Road level crossing. The smaller building to the left is the Royal Dock Chambers, behind which was the Railway Bakehouse.

came over to try to clean me up. Dad was cross. Before he could continue his deliveries, he had to take me home to get me washed and changed.

After that I stayed in the van on the Docks run. Some of those lumpers and fish merchants became good friends and would sometimes slip my Dad some fresh fish and me a bag of sweets.

The refreshment rooms on the railway stations were interesting places. When I go to one of those preserved railways, I always head for the Refreshment and Waiting Rooms. Most were of similar build and layout, with a counter on one side and a few tables in the middle of the floor. Around the sides of the room were 'booths' – bench type seating with a table in the middle. They would invariably be full. When the railways put this side of their business out to tender, much of this tradition was lost because everything was modernised and sanitised. No more home

baking. Everything, including sugar and salt, was in plastic bags. It was more healthy, but less interesting and tasty.

I was able to help Dad carry things into the railway station Refreshment Rooms and usually came out with 'something'. At first I was known just as 'Sid's son', but by the time I was eleven or twelve, I was quite well-known as Ken. From then on it was often Dad who stayed in the van while I did the donkey work.

Apart from the work Dad did for the bakehouse, he often worked in the Refreshment Rooms for a bit of extra money. He also worked in the saloon on the ferries that took people from the Royal Dock Basin to Spurn Point and back on afternoon and evening trips at the weekends. The food served on those ferries was supplied by the same bakery and was always popular.

The trips themselves were always well patronised because the ferry boats were paddle steamers and the engine room was easily seen through glass panels. The ships – Lincoln Castle, Tattershall Castle and Wingfield Castle, were also owned by the railway company, and normally operated between New Holland and Hull. If you wanted to travel from Grimsby to Hull, you bought a railway ticket and travelled to New Holland by train and then completed your journey by ferry.

The main attractions for me at the railway stations were the huge steam engines. I have no technical knowledge or expertise and that side of it has never interested me to any great extent. But just seeing those giants of the tracks moving and shunting always held a fascination for me.

When the bakery closed, Dad still had some 'working life' left but he was too old for 're-training', so for the last few years he worked as a goods porter at the Central Market Depot. He hated every moment and retired on his sixty-fifth birthday, a Tuesday in 1963, because he could not bear to go to work another day.

In one way, it was a sad end to an otherwise happy working life, but he still had travel privileges and went out a lot on day trips with my Mum.

Ken Craggs

Shops on Corporation Road

The shopping needs of the 'Marsh-ites' were catered for by Corporation Road, from Charlton Street to the Corporation Bridge. Every type of shop was along this road, including the pub 'Kingies', a pawnbroker – most essential, and of course a florist – for marriages and funerals. There was also a school, Armstrong Street for infants, boys

and girls eleven years and upwards, separated of course.

George Morton

Counting the Coupons!

After the war, I can remember queuing up for a meal at Lord Street Methodist Church, and Mother presenting coupons at the newsagents for sweets. We always had mint rock or fruit gums! Sometimes I asked if we could have different sweets but Mum would say that she would use too many coupons at one time!

Eileen Riggs

Clock Watching!

I joined the Yorkshire Electricity Board in 1958. Latterly in my employment, after the resident watch and clockmaker Horace Willmer retired, I took over the maintenance of the prominent clock tower above the Cleethorpes Electricity Shop, close to Isaac's Hill. This is a listed 'art deco' building dating back to the 1930s.

David L. Riggs

Dobson's Errand Boy

Starting Work

Dobson's the ironmonger's in Freeman Street, was established in 1892 by John Hedley Dobson. He originally had a business in Albert Street, where he lived. He was a plumber and tinsmith. I joined this business

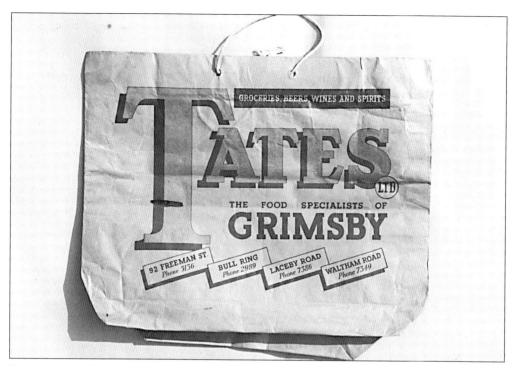

Tate's name is still seen in various places around Grimsby, though the firm is now part of a larger chain. This is a bag you would have put your groceries during the thirties.

in 1945 as an errand boy at £1-5s-0d per week, having left school hoping to become a joiner. With so many men away at the war, the firm was not taking apprentices. The next best thing was to sell joinery tools.

Being an errand boy was a miserable job in the bad winters we had in those days. The snow was so thick that the footpaths had to be cleared daily. The snow was piled two foot high in the gutters, making the roadway very narrow. It took weeks to thaw. No prizes for guessing who cleared the snow!

Peacetime

The war was just finishing, though rationing continued for much longer. We were allowed three quarters of a pound (340 grams) of sweets per month. This was quite hard on a sweet-toothed lad. There was a young lady who worked at Dobson's who had connections with a sweet shop. Every Friday lunch time she shared her ill-gotten gains with me. Another luxury was fresh fruit. If we were lucky we got one pound of bananas per month.

Although the war was nearly over, stock was still in short supply. Every new consignment was eagerly opened to see what it contained. This was part of my job; I was like a kid in Aladdin's cave! There were pots and pans, joinery tools, screws, nails, knives and fittings of all kinds. And, of course, locks. Dobson was one of the main locksmiths in Grimsby. The most unpopular delivery was nails – two tons in one hundredweight bags. These were barrowed down the passage at the

The Ladysmith Road premises of Glenton's Wonder Bakery in 1958.

rear of the workshop into the tinners' shop. In the ceiling was a trapdoor which opened to reveal a block and tackle. The bags were hoisted into the stockroom above.

Another of my jobs was to restock the shelves in the shop. One of the heaviest was to refill the nail boxes. Up and down the stairs I went; I must have walked miles. Sometimes I struggled with a hundredweight of sandstone. This was sold in small pieces which were used for cleaning the old-fashioned doorsteps.

Busy Days

I preferred Tuesdays, Fridays and Saturdays. These were market days. All hands were required behind the counter. To say we were busy would be an understatement. Most of the customers were housewives. We sold everything from a pan scrub (scourer) to a dolly stick and dolly tub. Trade would ease up towards 4.30 p.m. and it would pick up again about 5 p.m. Freeman Street would become a sea of bicycles. The dock workers were on their way home! This was their opportunity to purchase whatever they needed for their DIY, though we did not use that term in those days. They bought anything from a pair of hinges to a pound of six-inch nails.

There were no official tea breaks in those days. A mug of tea was left on a shelf hidden from the view of customers. Sometimes we had to pretend that we needed to pass this shelf, otherwise we would never get the tea. Usually, by the time we drank it, it was cold.

The second year I worked there, the government decreed that all employees would get a second week's holiday with pay. That was like winning the pools.

Memorable Customers

Some strange characters came into the shop. One of our regular customers was a mattress manufacturer. On entering the shop one day he threw a hammer at me. I jumped back in panic but he just laughed. It was made of rubber!

Another regular customer was a joiner who smoked herbal tobacco. We could smell it when he was a hundred yards away. It was marvellous how quickly the staff could disappear leaving 'muggins' (me!) to serve him.

Quite a lot of foreign seamen came in. The sale was often done with hand signals. One of the most difficult was performed by a very large man. He kept making a lot of sweeping movements. It turned out that he was a ship's cook and he wanted a large carving knife. I felt much better when he had left the shop with the knife well wrapped in brown paper.

I went home quite excited one night; we

A Morris Commercial van in Hewitt's yard off the Bull Ring in 1957. Standing next to the van is the late Herbert Bradley.

had had a black man in. I knew that there were black people, but it was the first time that I had seen one.

Difficult Deliveries

Cycle deliveries to the villages surrounding Grimsby were impossible. The answer was to use the horses and carts that were stationed in the Bull Ring on market days. These were known as carriers. Very often I would cycle to the Bull Ring precariously balancing a tin bath or a dolly tub on my bike. Sending by carrier would have cost my boss sixpence per item. A disadvantage of riding the bike was that the load sometimes exceeded my weight.

Progress does not stand still. Eventually my carrier bicycle was replaced by a motor van. This van must have been one of the first ever to have been made. We were never very sure about its age. My boss was so harassed by the uncertainty of it starting first thing in the morning, that we approached it together. We usually got it started, but sometimes it took a long time. I was excited – suddenly I was a driver! The best part was that I kept dry.

Who says they were the 'good old days'?

Polish Customers

The well-known Weelsby Woods Park was used as a prisoner-of-war camp during the Second World War. Towards the end of the war it held Polish soldiers. We were never sure whose side they were on. I think they were detained for their own protection. Once a week, two Polish officers would come to the shop to purchase handles and snap catches for brief cases. Apparently, the Poles were renowned for their handicraft skills.

Where they acquired the leather and other materials is still a mystery. I can recall the Poles to this day. They were quite elegant in their smart uniforms, clean and well presented, and possibly in their forties. They obviously ate very well. To me they seemed quite plump. I seem to remember that they always smelt of some sort of scent. Their manners were impeccable and they spoke good English. When they could not make us understand, they gestured or drew diagrams on paper. On completion of their business, they would bow and salute. They were a pleasure to serve. They made quite an impression on me as a young lad.

Two Characters

I remember most clearly two men returning to their jobs from the war. Alf Blow was a locksmith and Norman Altoft was a tinsmith. Both had been fitters in the RAF. These men were heroes to a young lad.

I used to watch Alf make keys – he was a dab hand at it. His talents were revealed when a local firm frequently lost their safe key. How he managed to make a key to open that safe without a pattern I shall never know.

Norman Altoft could make anything out of metal. His workshop had a small coke stove which heated the soldering irons. I used to slip into the workshop on a winter's day and watch fascinated as he soldered. The solder used to run like water. I never worked out how he knew the irons were at the right temperature. My boss always knew where to look when he wanted me!

Norman was a keen motorcyclist. The love of his life was a Norton 500 cc. He kept the machine immaculate. Occasionally he came to work on it. The roar of the powerful engine reverberated down the brick passageway.

I was always trying to get Alf and Norman to tell stories about their wartime exploits. Like most ex-servicemen they never boasted about their deeds. Instead they kept me entertained with their silly stories and silly voices. It was like a premature Goon Show. Every chance I got I would quote the first line of some piece of poetry or a silly saying, hoping to set them off. Sometimes it worked, sometimes not. I might say, 'I'm in the family way.' Back would come the response, 'You're in everybody's way!' I would complain that I could not find the end of some curtain wire. Back would come the laconic remark, 'Someone's cut if off!' It sounds corny now, but not fifty years ago, when humour was in short supply.

A customer might ask if he could wait for a key to be cut. Alf's quick reply would be, 'Certainly. As long as you wait at home!'

A more serious piece of advice was, 'If you cannot find what you want, make it'. Many times I have done this and I always think of Alf Blow.

Reflecting

I often wonder why the first job I had, which lasted only four years, has had such a lasting impression on me. It must have been because of the people I worked with. All were such wonderful characters.

The shop is now used by a charity. Every time I walk past, the old memories stir. I still think of it as 'J.H. Dobson,

Already two shops are empty as the town centre is remodelled, but R. C. Johnson hangs on. Butchery Lane (left) is closed as demolition begins in the Bull Ring.

"The latest farm equipment...soon all farms will have one." A Fordson tractor and driver ready for work in the Grimsby area, but where and who?

Ironmonger'. It's not, it's just a ghost from the past.

Why did I leave? I got an invitation I could not refuse – two years in HM service. This was a totally new experience. When I was demobbed, Dobson's owner asked me to go back. I declined; the grass is always greener on the other side of the fence. Perhaps I should have gone back. If I had, my memories would have been different. Memories can't be taken away from you.

David Edwards

Buying on the 'never-never'

I went with my Mum to buy a radiogram from one of the shops in Victoria Street. It was a big polished wooden thing on legs with a heavy lid. Mum couldn't afford to pay for it outright, so she bought it on hire purchase. Some people called it the 'never-never'. She went to the shop every week to pay them some more money. It took her two years to pay for it, and Dad said 'never-never again'! She did buy other things on hire purchase because we wouldn't have had them otherwise, but she told us not to tell our friends how we paid for them.

Maureen Thompson

Paying by wire!

On the corner of Freeman Street and Garibaldi Street, next to the cinema, was a branch of the Co-operative Society. I used to be enthralled by the money machine, and would happily watch that while by mother did her shopping. The sales assistant would take your money and place it with details of your purchases into a container that connected to wires suspended from the ceiling. She would pull a handle to send the container whizzing along the wires to the pay office. Within a couple of minutes, the container would come whizzing back across the ceiling to the correct sales counter, carrying receipt and change for the assistant to give to the customer. During the wait, the assistant had been passing the time of day very pleasantly with the customer, while she tidied up the counter. I don't remember seeing the system in use on a busy day, but I imagine there would have been a lot of waiting for the container to return.

Betty Fox

CHAPTER 6

Street Life

VICTORIA STREET, GRIMSBY.

Victoria Street with the Savoy cinema on the left. The Savoy became the Gaumont, the Odeon and finally Focus. Note Gough and Davy's music shop on the right.

Bing Sings

One of Grimsby's most memorable post-war characters was 'Bing'. He was always singing as he went about his business up and down Corporation Road – in the style of Bing Crosby, hence the name. We never knew his proper name, but people knew <u>him</u>, and he was always happy.

Roger Marsh

Houses blown up

In 1956 there was a gas explosion in Park Street which demolished two houses.

Doug Wise

Almost lured away!

Once a man approached my brother and me down The Lane (Ladysmith Road). He

Harry Edmonds the coal merchant outside 52 Cooper Road.

lurked around there for a time. He was a 'funny' man. He was trying to lure us away. 'I'll give you sixpence if you'll follow me', he said. We said, 'Thank you', took the sixpence, and then ran the other way. We never did tell Mum where we got that sixpence from. It was a lot of money in those days. We had threepence each and didn't let on.

Anne Harris

Living near the Lane

I was born in 1943, so my earliest memories are of the post-war years of the late 1940s. I was the youngest of four, one boy and three girls. We lived in an end terrace house behind a shop, where my family had moved to when our house in Edward Street was bombed when I was four months old. My parents rented our new house from a Mr Flynn. It had a big garden where we used to play. The house was in the old part of Ladysmith Road, which then ended just past Columbia Road at what was known as 'Bagley's Corner', named after the removal firm who had premises there. Beyond this point was a track known as 'The Lane', with fields on either side, which led up to Weelsby Woods. Even after it was made into a proper road with buildings along its length, and the name 'Ladysmith Road' officially applied to it, local people still called it 'The Lane'.

Just around Bagley's Corner was a passageway that led past Granville Tours' bus depot and down into Welholme Road, along which we walked to school. We always called this 'the hill' for obvious reasons. This area has been taken over by Birds Eye, so there is no public access now.

Lorna Osbourne

Ladysmith Road Memories

To go to Welholme School, we walked from Cooper Road corner down a cutting at the back of Granville Tours. Boys were always horrid to us girls down the cutting. It came out at the bottom of Welholme Road. The Metal Box Company had premises near there, and in the late fifties, a huge fire destroyed much of their premises. There was an ice skating rink on Ladysmith Road, but it closed and was turned into a Nibbit's factory. Behind Salverson's was the schools' playing field.

Linda Oxley

Gutter Walker

There was an old lady who always walked in the gutter. She was small, thin and dressed in black. We kids felt in awe of her, and sorry for her. Many times a beat policeman put her back onto the pavement with a warning about the traffic. Within yards she was back in the gutter. The story was that her husband had been killed by a vehicle mounting the pavement, and she could not accept it. We wondered how long it would be before she too was hurt by a passing vehicle.

Roger Marsh

An attractive town to Visit

One regular 1960s visitor to the town remarked on how attractive the entry routes were. Scartho Road, Louth Road, Yarborough Road, Laceby Road, as well as others like Weelsby Road, had been carefully planted with suitable trees, and provided a green and leafy welcome to many visitors. Unfortunately progress (and financial constraints) decree that the modern main route

The much missed Corn Exchange in Old Market Place.

The site of the Corn Exchange, with Chambers' shop boarded up on the right. The curved block of shops was built when the tight corner from the Bull Ring into Victoria Street was remodelled.

passes through an industrial estate with its many and varied sheds, office blocks and factory unit… and no trees.

Brian Leonard

Only Organic

Mr Cammack from Laceby brought fresh vegetables to us every Friday by horse and cart during the thirties. No need to advertise organic vegetables then, we all knew they were organic! As ours was then the last house in our avenue, Mr Cammack placed a canvas nosebag on his horse, to give it an enjoyable feed. On moving off, the horse left its 'calling card' and I was delegated to fetch the brush and shovel, the contents of which were to be used around our rose bushes!

Jean Ashling

Keeping the Streets Clean

Bert was our street cleaner. We never knew his surname. He pushed a handcart for the rubbish and it carried his brush and shovel. He did a good job keeping the roads clear of paper and other rubbish that people just threw onto the street. There wasn't as much 'throwaway' material then (in the fifties) as there is now. Eventually, his job was to be modernised. The new collecting carts were electrically driven by on-board batteries and travelled at a walking pace. Sticking out in front was a handle that controlled the power and the steering. Bert refused to have one because they were intended to cover three handcart rounds. How far can a man walk in a day sweeping up rubbish, even if his cart is electrically driven? Bert stayed with his handcart only a few more months before he retired.

Annie Hewson

Gambling Habits

Houses were built mostly in straight streets with front doors opening onto the road. The women sat on chairs or stools, gossiping at their front doors in the summer. Betting was illegal for the working class, but there was always one particular lady who took the bets. Children used to sneak their father or mother's horse racing bet to her, a screwed up paper with the 3d or 6d coin in the middle. People thought they would be less suspect.

At the end of Gilbey Road was a track that led up to the Humber bank. Men would meet down there to play 'pitch and toss', because that was illegal too. Strangers walking or cycling by were looked at very suspiciously.

'Housey Housey' (which was later popularized as Bingo) was also illegal but games used to be organized in certain houses always with a watcher or a guard.

Women belonged to a 'pinny club' where, for a penny a week, when their turn came round they were given a new pinny (apron, or pinafore).

George Morton

Name Changed

At the junction of Cambridge Road and Chelmsford Avenue, a new road – Ely Road – was built a hundred yards or so towards Bargate. Where it stopped was a hedge and then a field of cows. Later, sensibly, the road was extended to link up with Westward Ho! but confusion ensued when the road had a different name at its two ends. Eventually

Milton Road and Leighton Grove residents enjoying their street party to celebrate the Coronation on 13 June 1953.

The Bull Ring toilets viewed from Old Market Place, the shops having been demolished. The new Church House is being constructed (behind the shed), and on the right is the Crest Hotel.

someone at the council realized and the whole length became Westward Ho! Hence the plate which reads 'Late Ely Road'.

Patricia Bradley

A Smelly Way

The passageway that links Doughty Road with Catherine Street passed under the London railway line and cut through the town's gasworks, which were demolished in 1964. The passageway also ran alongside the Municipal Electricity Generating Station. The subway under the railway line had a very low roof, and the walls seemed always to be wet. There was an odd bend in it so you could not see straight through. It was lit by one solitary bulb – not a place to 'dally' in! The whole area smelt strongly of coal gas, as you

would expect. Incidentally, 'Catherine' had an odd local pronunciation, not the normal way of the girl's name. There was equal emphasis on the two syllables, the second being pronounced as the German river, so people said 'Kath-Rhine Street'.

Betty Williams

Fascinated by the Pagoda

I remember walking up Littlefield Lane to where the Cricketers public house is now. This used to be a rough lane with hedgerows. But what sticks out most in my mind is a building we used to call the pagoda. It was visible among the trees and we used to stand and look in awe at something which was totally out of place in the overgrown gardens. My memory of the absolute details is not as clear as it might be, but I remember walking to look at this building each time we came on visits. When we finally moved to live in Grimsby in 1960, it had gone and more modern houses had been erected in its place.

Sandra Leonard

Street Activities

The advantage of there being few cars on the roads was that it was safe to play out in the street. There were seasons in our games. I can't remember which order they came in through the year, but there were skipping, hopscotch, marbles, whip and top, and team games like hide and seek.

Horses and carts were used by traders to deliver goods, and there was a greengrocer called Mr Stubbs who had a grey horse known as Dinky. Mr Stubbs used to let us ride on his cart and sometimes let us have the reins to 'drive'. There was a general shop halfway down our block, owned by a lady called Mrs Overan, where we used to spend our sweet rations.

Lorna Osbourne

A Lovely Smell!

To visit my aunt in Willingham Street, I used to cross the railway at Holme Street, then go into Sixhills Street and pass Tickler's jam factory. What a treat that rich fruity smell was!

Peter Hewitt

Being Grandma's Eyes

My first memory of going for walks was with my maternal Grandma, who had poor eyesight because of glaucoma. It was before I

Contractor E. Robert White laying asphalt about 1920. Notice the RAOB Club and the Co-op buildings.

Children on a 'Town Walk' along the track bed of the railway line to Boston and London seen from the old bridge known as Peak's Tunnel. Peak's Parkway now uses this route.

started school, so must have been when I was about four. I would act as her eyes and tell her if it was safe to cross the road. There was little traffic in those days but if anything was coming, I would stand in front of her, hold out my arms and bar her way.

Lorna Osbourne

Snowballing Fun

One winter when we had a good fall of snow, I remember my friends loading a sledge with snowballs and going along both sides of Sutcliffe Avenue from Second Avenue to First Avenue, throwing snowballs at people's doors. Thankfully in those days the doors were wooden. How naughty and foolish, because if we had been seen, our parents

would have been told – we were from the area and everybody knew who lived where. Nowadays we might be classed as hooligans. We just thought we were having fun and did not hurt anyone.

David Bradley

Cheap Fuel – Cheaper Transport

We lived on Willingham Street, near to Catherine Street, where the entrance to the gasworks was situated. Often on a winter Saturday morning, we could see a procession of people walking into the gasworks entrance with an old pram, a wheelbarrow, a sack barrow, or just a set of pram wheels. For a modest sum, they could buy a bag of coke, which was what remained when coal had gone through

The photographer was standing on the track bed of the abandoned London railway line near to the passage that linked Doughty Road and Catherine Street. In the distance is the multi-storey car park at the side of Doughty Road.

the process to make town gas. Coke was not as good a fuel for the fire as coal, but it was cheaper and had a lovely red glow. The gas-making process was a much more efficient way of using the many chemicals that constitute coal.

Betty Williams

Whipped by the Driver

Traffic was almost non-existent down Armstrong Street except for Dixon's steam lorries. These fascinated us children. We liked to see the chimney smoke as they chugged up the incline towards the mill. Also, the men called 'deal carriers', who would run along and up planks with another man on their shoulder stacking the wood as high as twenty feet (six metres), to be stored and weathered. The long planks were taken

from the wood yards for delivery by 'cut carts', which lengthened as required. Left protruding at the rear was a long square beam across which we used to lay to sneak a ride. As we so lay, our rear ends were exposed to the driver, who, leaving his horse to plod along, dropped off and delivered blows with his whip to our rear ends.

George Morton

Grimsby's Biggest Ever!

Once a year, though I can't remember at what time of year, there was a parade that went right through the town. It was called the 'Biggest Ever' and it really was. There were decorated floats, clowns, people riding funny bicycles, and everyone dressed up and colourful – very similar to the parade that goes through Cleethorpes in the summer today (but without the marching bands). However, when you are small, everything appears so much bigger. Everybody used to turn out to watch that parade and we stood with our parents for what seemed like hours until the last float had passed by. I think the collection that they made was for the Grimsby Hospital.

Lorna Osbourne

New Houses Built

When I was a boy, there were fields from Hainton Avenue to Love Lane Corner, apart from one cottage.

One house was built in 1924 at the corner of Recto Avenue. My father, Ben Wilkinson, built six detached houses on Weelsby Road, beginning at Hainton Avenue. We moved into one on the other corner of Recto Avenue in 1928. There was a lovely view from our front window on to the fields opposite, where there was at least one donkey.

This view was spoiled with the building of the Hainton Inn and the Ross Sports Club. The club was set well back so we could still see the beautiful trees of Weelsby Woods. We see less of the trees now that a housing estate has been built on the club site.

On Laceby Road in 1932, I remember sitting on the roof rafters of a house we were building on the corner of Carnarvon Avenue. From there I could see the Lincolnshire Show, which was held on land behind Laceby Road, owned by Sir Alec Black. Hereford School now stands on that land.

After returning from Army Service, we joined other building firms in extending the Nunsthorpe Estate over open land. The borough architect, Wilfred Ingham, had an eagle eye when inspecting the properties!

Norman Wilkinson

No Coal for the Boilers

I remember 1947 as the year of the Great Snow Fall. There was a coal shortage, so we were sometimes sent home from school. I believe it was about this time that the traffic island at the junction of Sutcliffe Avenue and Second Avenue was being constructed.

David Bradley

The roundabout at the junction of Sutcliffe and Second Avenues. The two houses in the centre are 45 and 47 Second Avenue.

Houses in course of construction on Weelsby Road in 1928. Note the trolley wires on the left showing Hainton Avenue corner. Recto Avenue is to the right of the fourth house.

The Cubs who met at St George's Methodist Church in 1951/2.

Gaiety Humour

The major dance venue of the fifties and sixties was the Gaiety Ballroom, at the corner of Willingham Street and Wintringham Road. Often big name bands or touring celebrities would play. One evening, winners of a national competition treated us to a display of modern dance techniques. Their steps were perfect, but the female dancer's face was fixed rigid in a concrete smile. Some comedian created a laugh with the comment, 'Bet she spends more time practising her smile than she does her dancing!'

Alan Smith

Seasons

(With apologies to Solomon)

There was a season for everything:
A season for marbles and a season for hop-
scotch;
A season for faggies and a season for
conkers;
A season for stilts and a season for roller
skates;
A season for strutting and a season for
cricket;
A season for jacks and a season for hoops;
A season for love and a season for want.

George Morton

Early Caxton's Players

Mum was one of the early members of the
Caxton's. She was in 'Fanny by Gaslight'
playing the maid. Dad was the electrician.
The Caxton's rehearsed in a church hall
on Freeman Street but their productions
were staged at the Plaza cinema on
Cleethorpe Road. This building was later
used by Huxford's as a shop selling electrical goods.

*Anne Harris, Linda Oxley
and Lorna Osbourne*

Happy Days (1920s)

For boys there was plenty of adventure and
pleasure. Sometimes two or three boys
would beg a blanket from Mam, then buy
some broken biscuits from grocers such as
Tates, the Maypole or The Monkey, Pig and
Pie shop. They would catch a tram to the
terminus at Welholme Road, then walk
along Hainton Avenue to where the
Hainton Inn is now. In those days this area
was all green fields, but Weelsby Road was
being built. After a few happy hours doing
what boys do – making a den with the blanket, eating the biscuits and playing games
– they would go back home.

Eric Robinson

The Coming of Television

Sales of television sets increased in 1953
because the forthcoming Coronation of the
new Queen was to be broadcast. My aunt,
Annie Newham, cleaned for a lady in
Roberts Street (facing Grant Thorald
Park), who allowed my aunt and myself to
watch the event on her new set. The screen
was perhaps only 25 cms wide, but the picture was clear enough for us. Little did we
realise the beginnings of the revolution we
were experiencing.

Brian Leonard

Looking across the Fields

I would often accompany my Granddad to
his allotment off Littlefield Lane. Looking
across the fields of cows, I could see a place
where many maroon and cream buses
passed rows of hedges. I worked out later
that it was the string of traffic islands
between Nun's Corner and Fryston Corner,
and the cows I saw would have been graz-
ing on the land now occupied by Hereford
School and the College.

Ray Woods

Scouts from the 16th Grimsby Troop in 1958, which met at South Parade Methodist Church. Back row left to right: P. Thornton, T. Miller, I. Retford and M. Morton.

Viewing the World!

I have vivid memories of the huge slide in Barrett's recreation ground. It took me ages to pluck up courage to climb the steps. After several attempts to mount them all, without returning to base, I finally found myself in the big cage at the top from where I believed I could see the rest of the world. The next challenge was to take the plunge down its very long and slippery slope. Once dared, it was brilliant. Countless children, my own included, must have felt the same and gone back for more time and time again. It was sad to see it go.

Sue Pannell

Entering the Kids Competition

Mum was brilliant at making fancy dress costumes so we always won the fancy dress competition on the Regal cinema stage. One of us was always the abominable snowman, and another dressed as the early bird. Mum loved dressing us up.

Anne Harris, Linda Oxley
and Lorna Osbourne

Not Converted to a Football Fan

My Dad took me to see Grimsby Town play at Blundell Park in the fifties when I was about twelve. I remember hearing a lot of

Humber Trinity football team in 1904-5. Front row, second from right is Victor Howe.

shouting from the standing male crowd, and seeing some of the racing about on the field. He took me twice more. I don't remember opponents or scores, but I do remember being relieved when he did not take me again. I could not understand what all the fuss was about.

Alan Smith

Watching Cricket

My father was a Yorkshireman and a great cricket lover, and I grew up listening to all Test Matches on the radio, and visiting Grimsby Town Cricket Club every Saturday afternoon, when the entrance was off Littlefield Lane. We always had an ice cream from the visiting van, a picnic and happy times with other regulars. Little did I know

then that I should come to watch my own son playing cricket there nearly forty years later.

Sue Pannell

Blowing Your Own Mouth Organ!

One year in the late fifties when the pantomime came to the Palace Theatre, all children in the audience were given a mouth organ. We were encouraged to suck and blow, but it played just FOUR notes!

Geoff Rudd

Street Games

There were seasons for playing street games: skipping, cigarette cards against the wall, and whip and top. We made our own and decorated them with chalks, so that when we were tired of the pattern we could rub it off and start again. We played two-ball against a wall.

Anne Harris, Linda Oxley
and Lorna Osbourne

Mariner's Fans!

In 1934 aged eight, I began watching Grimsby Town Football Club, reserves at first. One match was against Barnsley Reserves who played in red shirts and white shorts. After a violent thunderstorm, they were playing in PINK! There were no fast colours in those days, and the red shirt dye had run into the white shorts.

When I started going to the first team games, it was sixpence for ground entry plus threepence for the Cleethorpes stand. Dad had a season ticket.

By 1936 we had a good side which reached the semi-final of the FA Cup, playing Arsenal at Huddersfield. Being only ten, I was not considered old enough to go to the match.

In 1937, I went to Cleethorpes Girls' High School on Clee Road. Our needlework class

Grimsby Town A.F.C., 1938-39. From left to right back row: M. Atherton (trainer), N. E. Vincent, E. M Glover, G. J. Tweedy, J. B. Hodgson, H. Betmead, Mr R. D. Clarke (Director). Front row: J. Boyd, -?-Thomson, F. Howe, T. Jones, F. W. Crack, T. Buck. Circled: A. F. Hall (L), J. M. Beattie (R).

was on Tuesday afternoon – the same day Town had its replay matches. We could watch the traffic coming to the game. Our school afternoon ended at 3.45 p.m., so about eight of us regular supporters grabbed coats and satchels, and belted down Clee Road to Grimsby Road, caught a trolley bus, and got into the football ground at half-time. If we couldn't see, we stood on our satchels.

In 1939 Town once again reached the F A Cup semi-final, to be played at Old Trafford in Manchester. My family travelled in a booked railway coach, all members from Cleethorpes Transport Department. We just managed to get into the ground when they shut the gates. The capacity crowd of 77,000 is still the record for Old Trafford.

When the teams appeared, Town were defending the goal we were standing behind. There was one change to our team: George Tweedy had been taken ill, so young George Moulson was in goal. The rest of our team were: Vincent, right back; Hodgson, left back; Ginger Hall, right half (Captain): Betmead, centre half; Buck, left half; Boyd, outside right; Beattie, inside right; Howe, centre forward; Jones, inside left; and Crack, outside left.

The game kicked off and Grimsby Town played really well, then after twenty minutes an accident occurred. Our goalkeeper (Moulson) dived for the ball at the feet of Wolves' centre forward, and received a kick to his head. Both players were carried off on stretchers. Wolves' centre forward came back, but Moulson was taken to hospital. Town played the rest of the game with ten men and a reorganized team. There were no substitutes in those days. The crowd was very subdued for the rest of the game. We lost 5-0 but that didn't bother us. We were more concerned about Moulson.

Joyce Tyson

Enjoying fresh Tomatoes

My mother's father had an allotment on land which was at the end of Hamont Road (off Carr lane), though we walked to it from Queen Mary Avenue. He had two large greenhouses, and one small one in which he grew tomatoes. When his grandchildren went to the allotment they were allowed to eat the tomatoes in only the small greenhouse. Because we could eat as many as we wanted, I am now unable to eat tomatoes direct from the plants. However, I can eat them cut up. On the allotment he grew various vegetables and flowers.

David Bradley

Sights to Fascinate

Aeroplanes were a sight to make everyone look skywards, and were mostly biplanes. Some were employed by firms for advertising – either towing banners or for skywriting. Persil was a favourite one – the letters expanding if the wind wasn't too strong. Alan Cobham's Air Circus came to Waltham airfield bringing with it stunt fliers, an auto glider (a helicopter with a propeller in front instead of on the tail), and of course the Flying Flea, famous because of its tiny size.

George Morton

Practical Lessons

The Town Council of the late 1950s opened a unique youth project on a spare site in Armstrong Street. This 'Adventure Playground' gave children and teenagers the chance to build dens and other structures with adult supervision. Wood, nails, tools – and advice – were provided. There was room for everyone, and no 'aggro' that I can remember. We learnt how to handle the tools and materials by practical experience, and enjoyed the fun. Eventually it closed because the land was needed by its owners.

Terry Miller

Regular Cinema-Goers

Mum and I loved going to the pictures, and would queue for ages to see a film. Sometimes we would get a seat halfway through a film so we would have to stay put until we saw the other half later. If there was a good film showing at the 'Regal' on Freeman Street, we would take the number 7 bus to Central Market, walk across the railway bridge into Railway Street and then walk into Freeman Street. Many a time it would be dark when we journeyed home.

We especially enjoyed the Doris Day, Mario Lanza and Vera-Ellen films. These were always in colour!

I used to attend the Rex cinema matinee for children on Saturday afternoons. I would be given one shilling: sixpence for sweets and sixpence for entry to the two hour film show. We would watch a serial, a full-length film plus a cartoon and *Pathé News*. In 1953, the cinema held a competition for the Queen's Coronation celebrations. Children were encouraged to paint a picture of the Coronation. I won first prize – it was a £1 note! I was absolutely thrilled.

Eileen Riggs

Sixpence went a Long Way

On Saturday mornings, we went to the Children's Matinee at the cinema on Freeman Street. We had sixpence pocket money, which

One of the huts showed the Iron Age methods of construction.

would allow us to go on the bus along Pasture Street to Hainton Avenue, where we changed onto the number 10 route that took us along Freeman to the Regal near Garibaldi Street on the same ticket. That ticket was a return, so you could get all the way home again. There was enough money in the sixpence ($2\frac{1}{2}$p) to pay for our seat in the cinema.

Anne Harris, Linda Oxley
and Lorna Osbourne

Visiting the Chantry

My Grandma and Granddad would take us to the cinema in Chantry Lane as a treat. The film I most remember seeing is 'The River of No Return'. The Chantry building is still there but no longer used as a cinema.

Sandra Leonard

An Interesting Place to Visit

Up until the arrival of the Romans in this area in AD 48, there had been Iron Age settlements to the south of Weelsby Road. In 1970, John Sills and Gavin Kinsley discovered fragments of pottery on a site down Weelsby Avenue. It was decided to reconstruct the settlement there, and it opened in mid 1987. Three roundhouses were built, with a fourth sectionalized to show the construction methods. Many local schoolchildren discovered the delights of Iron Age life at the site.

Local vandals had other ideas. Arsonists destroyed the roundhouses in February and November 1989, and the settlement closed after only two years.

David Hall

A group of schoolchildren from Grange Middle School experience Iron Age life as it might have been, at the Weelsby Avenue site.

CHAPTER 8
Churches

St George's Methodist Church Primary Sunday School, c. 1958.

A Busy Church Life

We lived in Wharton Street off Macaulay Street, but belonged to the Baptist Church in Victoria Street, a good mile away. Sometimes we went three times on a Sunday. That meant a lot of walking – we had no car, of course!

The big event of the year was the Sunday School Anniversary. Scores of children were placed on a huge platform and read poetry, sang songs or hymns, etc. Everyone had something new for the occasion. I always had a new dress and ribbons for my long hair. Christmas parties were fun, too. We all sat at long tables and ate potted meat sandwiches, home-made cakes, jelly and ice cream. We played lots of games, my favourite being Musical Chairs. We went on outings too. Many a happy time was spent at Hubbard's Hills where we played games, followed by tea in the café near the car park. One year we

Flottergate Methodist Church, c. 1920. Many people have treasured memories of their time at their local church.

travelled by tram from Corporation Bridge to Immingham, where we played and had tea at a Methodist Church.

Eileen Riggs

An Important Influence

Flottergate Methodist Church, renowned for its architecture, was the spiritual home for many of the town's leading citizens. During my teenage years, we had a succession of Methodist Mayors who worshipped at Flottergate. Sir James Blindell attended Sunday School at Flottergate, and later became a Member of Parliament. Incidentally, my grandfather taught him in

Sunday School.

At the back of the gallery was a stained glass window to commemorate those who sacrificed their lives during the First World War. During the Second World War, pupils from the former Freeman's Grammar School used the building. It was also a centre for homeless people during the Blitz.

When St James' Parish Church was bombed in the early 1940s, the following Sunday was Mayor's Sunday. Because of the damage, Flottergate agreed to host the occasion. The choirs of Flottergate and St. James' united to pray for peace. The Mayor, Alderman Max Bloom, of the Jewish faith, was present together with his Rabbi.

When I was very young and in the Sunday School, we had a Superintendent who was very strict. If we misbehaved, we had to stay behind after the other pupils were dismissed. Only when we said 'sorry', would we be given permission to leave. Mr Elijah Crowson, a member of the congregation, kept an eagle-eye on the youngsters of the Sunday School. If we giggled during the prayers, he would poke us with his umbrella!

For many years, 'Teddy' Benton, as he was known, was the choirmaster. To be in Flottergate Choir, one had to undergo a voice test. I was terrified because 'Teddy' set such a high standard. However, I passed! Mr Benton had his own set of rules. If we were unable to attend choir practice on Friday evenings, we were not allowed to join in the singing of the anthem on the Sunday evening.

In my early twenties, I joined the 'King's Messengers', a mission band which toured the local Methodist Churches. Mr Fred Beasley was the leader, and one of his favourite hymns was 'Blessed Assurance'. On one occasion I was asked to give the address and I panicked! I was given an outline of the sermon, the text being 'Freely ye have received, freely give'. At midnight on the Saturday evening, I was trying desperately hard to find something that was relevant to the text. At that stage of my spiritual journey I wasn't sure just what I had received, and felt I had precious little to give. However, a few years later I became a local preacher in the Flottergate Circuit.

My parents were married in 1916 by the minister, the Revd Wilfred Callin, the writer of the hymn 'O Lord of every living thing, the maker of them all'. My father was in the Royal Naval Air Service, and was home on 48 hours' leave and married in Naval uniform.

St Martin's Church choir near to the Cenotaph in 1956.

St Martin's Church choir in 1952.

Some of the leading theologians visited Flottergate prior to the Second World War, including Dr William Sangster, Leslie Church and Leslie Weatherhead. Once, Kathleen Ferrier joined the Flottergate Choir for the rendering of Handel's Messiah.

Marjorie Barron

A Strange Notice

I remember seeing the Latin words 'Nota Bene' on a board outside a church in Freeman Street. I could never understand why they should inform everyone that there was 'not a bean' there!

Anne Harris

Choir at Old Clee

I joined Old Clee Church Choir in 1948. The choirmaster was Harry Neal, and the vicar was Canon Hill. There was a wooden hut in Clee Crescent, set back from the road, and on Wednesdays after the choir practice, I bought a fishcake and chips for 3d, or cod-cheeks and chips for 4d. On leaving church on dark nights, the choir-boys would have to look out for an owl, which would sometimes swoop down on us. Ironically, although Old Clee Church is in Grimsby, I had to catch a bus from the then new Windsor Road, which is in Cleethorpes. So I had to ask for an 'over-lap' ticket which was a purple colour with a diagonal red stripe.

David L. Riggs

Talking about Church

When I was swatting for my 'O' levels at Wintringham Boys' Grammar School, my form joined another for chemistry lessons. Someone asked the teacher how much homework we should do. He replied that he couldn't say how much should be done at weekends, 'because some of you have other commitments such as going to church'. At that there was a burst of laughter. As I greatly enjoyed attending Flottergate Methodist Church, the lad next to me took the full brunt of my anger. He didn't go to church but to my surprise he was interested in what I had to say.

Our conversation continued through that lesson and a few more. To cut a long story short, I failed chemistry 'O' level, even though it had been my best subject at school.

The lad started coming to my church and met a girl there whom he married. Both have been church members ever since.

As we had become friends at Littlecoates Primary School years before, I frequently describe him as 'my oldest friend' and I was delighted when he agreed to compile 'Grimsby Remembered'.

John D. Beasley

Church Moves

The Baptist Tabernacle in Victoria Street was sold to the brewers Hewitt Brothers in 1956, and the church moved to new premises in Laceby Road.

Doug Wise

Oldest friends. John Beasley and Brian Leonard, c. 1960.

The Young Leaguers of Heneage Road Methodist Church. Ruth Panton (back row, third left) was killed in the raid which destroyed the church.

Heneage Road Chapel Bombed

Heneage Road Chapel was situated down an alleyway or 'eight foot', between two houses in Heneage Road, facing Tasburgh Street. I was working in a shop at the corner of Ladysmith Road and Julian Street in 1940. Shop hours were long in those days – 8 a.m. until 8 p.m., and 9 p.m. on a Saturday. I had a one-hour break at teatime on a Saturday, but because I lived in Clifton Road I normally took sandwiches. My boss then was Mrs Beatie Walker who still lives in the same house in Miller Avenue. She had a baby and used to bring her in the pram to the shop on Saturdays.

The sirens sounded but people were used to them. Often it was a false alarm and no planes came over, especially in the daytime. We just carried on. All of a sudden we heard a plane and then a deep thud. An hour or so later someone came into the shop and told us that a bomb had dropped on Heneage Road Chapel.

Ruth Panton lived nearby with her father, the chapel's caretaker. She was a great friend of our family and we called her Auntie Ruth. She used to invite me to go for tea on a Saturday in my hour off as she thought it would be a break from the shop. I used to take Mrs Walker's baby with me in the pram. On the Saturday of the bombing, Mrs Walker asked me if I would mind not going to my auntie's as it was the Saturday before Christmas and we were busy in the shop. When I got home I found that Auntie Ruth was in hospital and her father was at our house. Ruth died two days later, and our Christmas was spent arranging her funeral. On Boxing Day, I went with my mother and Ruth's sister and brother-in-law from Nottingham to rescue things from the rubble. They gave me a box of tea knives for my help, which I still have.

The wooden hut was used for services for a while. I was married in it, but was not allowed to have photos taken as the war was still on. The church was never rebuilt, and the congregation split up.

Ivy Maidens

Serving in the Cubs

I joined the 7th Grimsby Cubs, at Weelsby Road Methodist Church, in 1949/1950. Incidentally, the Scout Leader, 'Skip' Jessop, married Akela, the Cub Leader, at Old Clee Church. We formed a Guard of Honour at their wedding.

In 1951 the scout and guide groups camped at Irby. Lord Rowallen visited the camp and we all had to wear kilts as a mark of respect, as he was Scottish!

David L. Riggs

Churches Amalgamated

With the redevelopment of the centre of Grimsby, and the decline in attendance, Flottergate Methodist Church had to go. Opened on 23 May 1880, with seating for 1069 people, it was too large to be viable, and closed on 15 November 1970.

St George's, a multi-purpose building, was constructed at the corner of Laceby Road and Second Avenue. It had opened on 24

May Queen Josie Riggall being crowned by Angela Wilkinson at St George's Methodist Church in 1958. Chief Attendant Jenny Gilleard (third right) looks on.

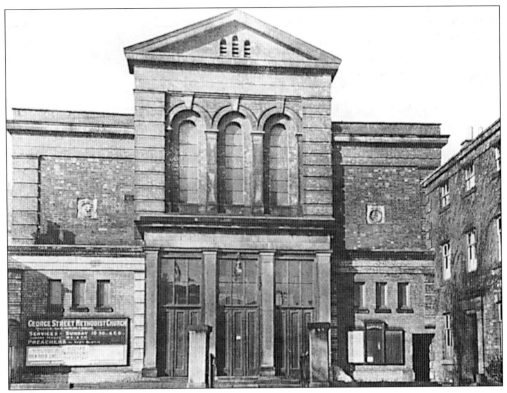

The solid front of George Street Methodist Church.

September 1953, being built from the proceeds of the sale of the George Street premises.

The reinstatement of Flottergate added a church to the site, which opened on 27 March 1971. Flottergate's magnificent pipe organ was installed in the new church.

Phyllis Chapman

Singing at St James' Church

I became a chorister at St James' Church in 1953. I achieved a choral scholarship, and therefore attended the church's school until 1958. I became Head Chorister in 1957 and was a member of the Church choir, boy and

then man, until 1976.

St James' Choir School was one of only five Parish Choir Schools in the country. Now it is unique.

David L. Riggs

Flottergate was Great

When my family moved from Hornsea to Grimsby in 1947, we attended Flottergate Methodist Church where I had many happy times, especially as a teenager when the Christian Endeavour Youth Fellowship, under the leadership of the Rev Alfred Wigley, arranged various activities. As captain of the football team I enjoyed playing on Barrett's Recreation Ground on Saturday mornings. We often played against lads who lived in the Brighowgate children's home, run by Mr and Mrs Thewlis whose son Peter was my best friend.

I still have my football shirt – a white one on which I used biro to write on the pocket 'Flottergate (Methodist) Christian Endeavour FC' with a large number 7 on the back.

As vice-captain of the cricket team, I recall with pleasure scoring a good number of runs. We often played in the People's Park. I still love batting, but I've lost the art of bowling.

The Flottergate youth club used to cycle to Humberston, Donna Nook, Immingham and other places. We often used to meet at the lions at the entrance to Weelsby Woods.

I had valuable public speaking experience on Friday evenings at the Christian Endeavour Youth Fellowship meetings. As a Methodist local preacher for over thirty-five years, I have preached a sermon in which I referred to giving a talk at Flottergate on my favourite Bible story – about Jesus chucking over the tables in the Temple. I admired the way that Jesus took action when he saw that something was wrong.

The first time I dialled 999 was when there was an explosion in the church boiler house. I was chatting to people in the schoolroom when suddenly the hatch blew across the room. I raced to the Bull Ring to phone for the fire brigade. If Nobby Clark, the friendly caretaker, had been in the boiler house he would have been killed. Thankfully he was talking to me in the schoolroom where plays and concerts were held and I used to take a bucket around to collect empty ice cream cartons.

When I was fourteen, I decided to give Christianity a trial run to see whether it was all that it was cracked up to be. For over

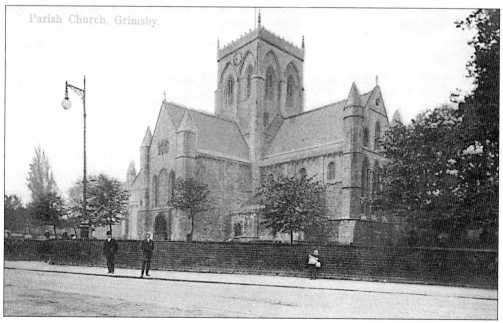

St James' Parish Church.

The Junior Section of the 4ᵗʰ Grimsby Boys' Brigade with blankets they had made for Oxfam, in July 1986. The blankets were received by Mrs Ivy Maidens, an Oxfam volunteer.

The 4ᵗʰ Grimsby Life Boy Team on 22 January 1956.

forty years I have considered that to be the best decision I have ever made.

Though Flottergate Methodist Church was demolished when the present shopping centre was built, its influence lives on. Years ago I wrote to the *Grimsby Evening Telegraph* suggesting that a plaque be erected where the church used to stand. I hope this book will encourage someone to organize it.

John D. Beasley

The Journeys of a Church Organ

The organ of St Paul's Church on Corporation Road had begun its existence in Dumfries Cathedral. It is now to be found in the Holy Trinity Collegiate Church at Tattershall, where it was taken when the West Marsh Church was closed prior to demolition in 1968.

Roger Marsh

Nine bungalows were built in Haycroft Avenue for elderly members of the local Methodist congregations, and were known as the Flottergate Benevolent Homes. The residents are seen enjoying an open-air service, c. 1960.

CHAPTER 9

Parks

A lovely view of swans and visitors enjoying the summer sunshine in People's Park early in the twentieth century. On the extreme left is the memorial to Alfred Henry Smethurst, JP, Grimsby's mayor in 1886 and 1887.

Silting

In 1700, the River Freshney was diverted through what is now the Duke of York Gardens to clear the haven (then Grimsby's dock, now the Alexandra Dock) of the increasing amount of silt. Two and a half centuries later, the Freshney itself was silting up, along New Haven Terrace and through the Duke of York Gardens. The water had dwindled to nothing more than a trickle, so narrow that we children could step across the 'river'. During one summer, the diggers came and removed many tons of evil-smelling ooze. Once cleared, the river filled again with water and became a picturesque asset that enhances the Gardens.

Incidentally, the original mouth of the river can still be seen on maps, if you follow the line of Gilbey Road to the river's edge.

Connie Ward

Walking to Bradley Woods

At one time there was a lovely walk from the corner of Second Avenue, near to where the Methodist Church is now. The land was used for allotments then, but people had a right-of-way across to Bradley Woods. During the summer we all took a picnic and spent a day at the woods. There was a swing in the middle of the wood. It was safe to walk in the countryside then.

Betty Clark

Played Football with Dad

Before my Dad opened his shop on a Saturday morning, we went to the Duke of York Gardens (known as the 'Boullee') to play football. Only once did he beat me. Years later my sisters let me into the secret that he used to let me win, but to stop me thinking I was a great footballer he decided to win one game.

John D. Beasley

A Popular Place to Play

The Ploggers was a playing field at the end of Weelsby Street, looking towards Weelsby Road. Where the name came from no one knows now. Lots of children loved playing there, sometimes catching newts in the stream. The circus and the May Fair were held on the waste ground beyond it each

The lake and one of the bandstands in People's Park.

year. We could walk to Old Clee Church near Love Lane Corner.

Anne Harris, Linda Oxley and Lorna Osbourne

Enjoying new Skates

I remember buying a pair of ice skates for a penny from lost property at school when I was 11. I didn't know when or where I should be able to use them, but I just wanted to be like my big sister who went with her friends every Saturday morning to the skating rink in Ladysmith Road. I wasn't allowed to go, and anyway my sister and her boyfriend did not want a little sister in tow! My chance came when the People's Park lake froze over – luckily before I grew out of the skates – and everyone seemed to have the same idea. I wonder now how the frozen lake managed to support us all but we reached the island and back to the side safely. This is something we would not be able to do today.

Sue Pannell

Lost Ship

During a visit to the People's Park, I was sailing a battleship which my uncle had made for me. Suddenly, a swan pecked the string and the ship sailed away on the lake. My Dad told two park-keepers who paddled a canoe and rescued my ship, which I still have.

David Sellers

Accident at the Park

One day in 1949, I went with my sisters to Sidney Park from Ladysmith Road. I was only six, Linda was seven and Anne was nine. We walked up to Fiveways, along Queen Mary Avenue and into Sidney Park. We thought nothing of it, and we were allowed to go. Anne was trying to get on the rocking horse when some boys pushed it. She got stuck under it and broke her leg. Somebody 'pagged' her home on a bike – was it Jeffrey Saunders? Linda and I ran all the way home with her. It's amazing to think that we were safe to go so far and were never assaulted.

Lorna Osbourne

The wedding of Albert Victor Howe and Emma Tutty on 24 August 1910. The service was held at All Saints' Church.

Losing our Home in a Raid

Our house at 97 Edward Street was double-fronted with a line of trees by the gate. The front room was taken up by a huge shelter – I think it was a Morrison. We used to play in that room in the daytime. There was no furniture in there because of the huge great shelter.

When the sirens went in July 1943, we were taken and put in the shelter. Our house was hit and All Saints' Church in Heneage Road was hit during the same raid.

Some old folks from number 91 (Victor and Emma Howe) were the only ones who came to see if the house was damaged. We spent the night in their house and after that we went to a centre in Hainton Avenue. It might have been the church on the corner of Bradley Street. We were billeted with some people called Clayton who seemed to have hundreds of children of their own. The Claytons were nice people and lived in Fairmont Road, but there were always many children there. Mum went out to look for accommodation for us and she found a house in Ladysmith Road. The people who owned it (Mr Flynn and family) were trying to keep it to make money on it, but they were forced into letting us have it. We liked living there and stayed until 1961.

Anne Harris

The Mystery of the Missing Airman

At Runnymede stands a memorial to British and Commonwealth airmen lost during the last war. One of the 20,455 names is that of Kenneth Barton Smith, who came from Grimsby. He was shot down over the English Channel during a Battle of Britain skirmish in August 1940.

Kenneth was the only child of Maria, a lady-in-waiting to the Princess Royal, and Herbert Smith, a radio operator from a P&O liner. During their years in Grimsby they lived at 116 Yarborough Road.

After attending Wintringham Grammar School, Kenneth began work with a London insurance company, and joined the Royal Air Force Volunteer Reserve in 1938, which involved attending evening classes and weekend air training. Called up and as number 7854895, he passed as a pilot, being posted to 257 Squadron at Hendon. There were problems in the squadron, losses mounted and morale plummeted.

Initially the squadron had Spitfires, but these were replaced with the less glamorous Hurricanes, and the squadron moved to Northolt on 1 July 1940.

On 7 August 1940 a convoy of twenty merchant ships and nine escort vessels was passing the Isle of Wight from the River Medway, when it was attacked by enemy U-boats and JU 87 dive-bombers. Several squadrons were scrambled to go to the convoy's aid, including 257. During one of the engagements, Kenneth in aircraft R4094 was shot down. Back home in Yarborough Road, Kenneth's parents received news that he was 'missing, believed killed', with understandable shock. Soon after, PC Mitchell heard the German propagandist Lord Haw Haw announce on the radio that Sergeant Pilot Kenneth Barton Smith, number 7854895, was a prisoner-of-war. Mitchell passed on this good news to Kenneth's parents in Yarborough Road, but they heard no more. The Air Ministry had not been given this information, and there is nothing at the Public Record Office in Kew. It seemed strange that Lord Haw Haw would have the information if Kenneth had been shot down and presumably lost at sea.

It is certain that Kenneth was shot down in that fierce air battle on August 7, and there is no evidence that he was merely injured or rescued. Lord Haw Haw's brief was to spread bad news and false hope. We shall never know the full facts of the incident; the official report remains 'missing, believed killed'.

From information supplied by Marjorie Barron

School Attendance Affected

After a bad air raid on the East Marsh area, the attendance at Strand School was down to one third. It wasn't that the absentee children

A group of First World War soldiers. Front right is Albert Newham who lived at 195 Willingham Street until his death in 1946.

had all been hurt, but parents were reluctant to let them out of their sight after such a bad night.

Maureen Thompson

Celebrating VE Day

I can remember being in the outside Anderson Shelter in 1944 and then in the Morrison Shelter (inside the house) during 1944/5. I can just remember the VE party held on the grass in front of the houses facing the railway line, in Peaksfield Avenue in 1945. I can remember people standing on their bay windows taking photographs with their Brownie box cameras.

David L. Riggs

Elephants in the Sky!

We remember the barrage balloons in the sky. We thought they were elephants because we knew about elephants and they looked like elephants to our young eyes.

Anne Harris and Linda Oxley

Missing Thomas

Hitler's war changed many lives, including mine. In 1937 after Edward VIII's abdication in the previous December, I started going out with Thomas. I always called him that. I never shortened it; it didn't sound right. We became really good friends, and gradually our love for each other grew. War was looming, and he joined up, ready to fight for his country and to play his part. We got engaged on his first leave, hoping to marry a few months later. He was sent to France and I never saw him again. He was killed in the evacuation that led to Dunkirk. I met many other nice young men, but none of them matched Thomas.

Enid Webb

Experiences of an Air Raid

At 1.05 p.m., one Thursday in 1941 I had just left work – we had half days off in those days. I was turning from Cleethorpe Road into Freeman Street when I heard a loud droning sound. When I looked up there was a German bomber coming down the street just above roof height. All the cyclists coming down 'Freemo', myself included, threw our bicycles down and dived into passages – the nearest me was by the shoe shop. We heard bombs going off, and when it was quiet, we came out. What a mess we saw. Burgens the grocer's at Kent Street corner had been hit and people killed. Harris the jeweller, which was nearly opposite, had its windows blown out, and rings and watches were scattered all over the pavement. I helped to clear up the mess because my friend worked there.

On arriving home in Second Avenue, I discovered that my Mam knew nothing about it, as the sirens had still not sounded. The plane had gone on and machine-gunned Waltham School children. In the evening my friend and I went to the Regal Cinema (later the ABC) in Freeman Street. When the siren went, we came out and never rushed home so quickly. When

I went to work the next day, I saw a lot of shops on Cleethorpe Road that had been bombed out.

Betty Clark

The Air Raid in June 1943

I spent the whole period of the raid on the night of 13-14 June in our Anderson shelter, so the severity did not become apparent until we came out at the sound of the 'all clear'. The sky was lit up with the glow from the fires, from bright orange to dark red.

Our neighbours stopped at our house, having been for a walk to Old Clee. They said Weelsby Hall was on fire. We could hear explosions, and our neighbours suggested it was tins of paint in the Strand Street paint store exploding. We discovered that it was anti-personnel bombs – the notorious butterfly bombs.

Father said that things looked bad and he had better report to his Fire Station. He put on his uniform and rushed off. He spent the night attending to fires all over the town, and getting reserve equipment out of store. When he returned home in the morning, he warned us to beware as there were a lot of small unexploded bombs around.

As I delivered telegrams around the town, I soon realized how bad the raid had been. Many of the anti-personnel bombs had already been discovered and surrounded with sandbags. Traffic and pedestrians were carefully passing by. In Grimsby Road there was one right in the middle of the road. I watched a trolley bus slowly drive round it, when a small boy came running along the middle of the road and leaped over the bomb! As I returned to the post office yard, a bomb in South St Mary's Gate exploded.

Owen Riggall (third from left) at the 1939 summer camp at Ferriby Sluice. Standing holding an axe is Captain Piggott Smith, with Mr Cerrino, Gordon Dobbs, Mr Bullen, Sergeant George Shirley and others.

A half filled sandbag was blown upwards and wrapped itself round the trolley bus wire. It hung there momentarily before dropping to the ground.

On the morning after the raid my Father was cycling past Eleanor Street when a bomb exploded. He went to the house where a bomb had lodged itself behind a wardrobe. When the door was opened it exploded and fatally injured a mother and her daughter.

Army Bomb Disposal personnel would pile additional sandbags round a bomb and clear the area before detonating it. They used both electric detonators and explosive fuses. When I lived in Carr Lane twenty years later, the mark the explosive fuses had made on the paving slabs could still be seen, especially in wet weather.

For months later the bombs were still being found and causing casualties. The fire service went round town searching for bombs lodged in the guttering and on roofs.

Norman Drewry

Working with Radar

Early in 1939 I was living in Louth, serving an apprenticeship as a baker and confectioner. I worked from 5 a.m. to 6 p.m. Monday to Friday, except Thursday, which was my half day when I finished at 2 p.m. My pay was five shillings per week.

As Thursday was my only totally free evening, I joined the Territorial Army, Number 4 Section of the Grimsby Company of the Lincolnshire Regiment, a searchlight unit based at Westward Ho!

Wartime Luftwaffe attacks were not confined to the experimental, but lethal, 'butterfly bombs'. On several occasions, freight trains received attention and were machine-gunned as they moved across the town. The twin bridges over Doughty Road bore evidence to at least one attack.

On 13 August 1939, we left Grimsby for a month at summer camp at Ferriby Sluice, South Ferriby. At 11 a.m. on a bright Sunday morning, we were listening to a car radio. It was 3 September and Neville Chamberlain announced that this country was at war with Germany. None of us realized just what that meant. One thing it did mean was that we did not return home at the end of summer camp.

In April 1940 volunteers were needed for a 'secret mission'. I volunteered and met two other Grimsby lads, Ted Fletcher and Les Stone. Ted's father, an alderman and magistrate, had a butcher's shop in Victoria Street near to Pasture Street corner, called 'The Monkey, Pig and Pie Shop'.

We were sent to Washington, County Durham, to train on a radio course. Having passed, we had to sign the Official Secrets Act, because we were being sent to train as Radar Operators. Radar was new, and very secret.

Once trained, we served at various locations before being posted to Ceylon. We were there for eight months, even working with the same radar equipment we had used when we were at Whitley Bay over a year before!

Owen Riggall

After a Raid

Altman's, where I worked, moved to the bottom end of Freeman Street. One Whit weekend, my boss and his wife went away, leaving me in charge. On the Sunday night we had a bad raid, so on the Monday morning I went down to see if everything was all right. It was difficult to get there as soldiers would not let people pass. They had put sandbags all over the road, and had set up a diversion, because 'Jerry' had dropped incendiaries and anti-personnel bombs.

Betty Clark

The Air Raid on 21 December 1940

The Saturday evening before Christmas we had just finished tea and were sitting round the fire listening to the wireless. There was a loud whistling noise and Dad pushed Mum and me into the cupboard under the stairs. As we went in there were three or four loud bangs. I said they were anti-aircraft guns and Dad agreed, but I noticed him shaking his head at Mum. The air-raid warning sounded a few minutes after the bombs had dropped. Mum and I went into the shelter and Dad changed into his ARP uniform and went to the Fire Station.

The all clear sounded soon afterwards, and when Dad arrived home he told us that the bombs had dropped in Heneage Road close to his Fire Station. One hit two terrace houses; the next hit a small chapel behind the houses, the others into the brick pit and caused no damage. A friend of Mum's lived in one of the houses and Dad said she had been hurt, but not badly, and was in hospital. When Dad returned from duty on Monday morning he told us that Mum's friend had died in hospital.

When Mum and I went to Church on Christmas morning, we saw the damaged houses. They were not completely destroyed, but had to be pulled down. Some of the firemen at Dad's station said that only three bombs had exploded and thought one had fallen into the brick pit and not gone off. Nothing was done about it. The brick pit was filled in after the war and now is a school playing field.

Norman Drewry

Hall Bombed!

Due to being scalded at home, I was convalescing in Weelsby Old Hall in June 1943. Incendiary bombs were being dropped all over Grimsby, resulting in the Hall being destroyed. All the patients plus their equipment were saved by Civil Defence workers. Sister K. Dennis, who was in charge, was honoured for her bravery. Prisoners from the prisoner-of-war Camp in Weelsby Woods were also drafted in to help. These were of Italian origin. My mother saw the fire from her house in Peaksfield Avenue and came and collected me and brought me home. I was sixteen months old.

David L. Riggs

Dressed for the Part

When I started working for the Post Office, I sometimes had to go to the Telephone Exchange. It was guarded by a postman who wore his Home Guard uniform and was armed with a rifle. This poor chap had lost an eye and a leg in the First World War, so he wore a patch over his eye and had an artificial leg. A pal said that if he had a parrot on his shoulder he could have guarded Treasure Island!

Norman Drewry

Wartime humour from Albert Newham, looking out of his garden Anderson shelter with nieces Kath and Gladys. Note the white rings around the barrels to help visibility in the blackout.

The Air Raid in July 1943

During the raid on the night of 12-13 July 1943 I was in the shelter with my mother, my father being on duty at his fire station. We were aware that bombs had dropped nearby, in fact the nearest was two streets away, in Algernon Street.

In the early hours of the morning there was a knock at our front door. My Auntie Ray said that she had been bombed out. She lived with my cousin Shirley in Deansgate, close to the bridge over the railway. It was very fortunate that they were in the shelter as a large piece of masonry had landed on the bed. When my father got home, he told us that our church, All Saints in Heneage Road, had been bombed. We also heard that the top

church, Saint James', had been hit too.

My morning duty started at 8 a.m., and as I cycled to work I was not aware of any damage until I reached Garden Street. Here I was shocked by the amount of damage to the small houses and shops - the road was covered in broken glass and slates. I had to carry my bicycle over the debris. When repairs were made to the Garden Street signal box the wooden base was replaced by a brick one.

There was no serious damage to the Post Office, just some windows blown in. I asked one messenger if there had been any damage to Albion Terrace in Cartergate. He said that the houses were all right when he had come past. It was only when I came off duty that I discovered that my grandparents' house in Albion Terrace had been damaged. Most of the windows had been broken and a huge piece of clay had come through the roof and slid down the bedroom wall leaving a muddy trace. Fortunately no one was hurt.

When I cycled by St James' Church I saw how much damage the two bombs had caused. The small houses and shops in St James' Arcade had suffered badly too. American soldiers were clearing broken glass from the windows of the American Red Cross Hostel, previously Turner's drapery shop. Later in the day I saw ARP workers lifting a person from the wreckage of a house in Dudley Street.

In Guildford Street the bombing left hardly a house undamaged. There were some UXB's (unexploded bombs) too. When a house was damaged or evacuated because of unexploded bombs, the whereabouts of the residents was chalked on the wall. I had two telegrams to deliver in Guildford Street. A policeman on duty at the corner took me down the street to find out the new addresses. At the first house I found only part of the front wall remained, but a new address was chalked on it. Another house had UXB chalked on it, and in a nearby crater I saw the fin of the bomb!

The Strand cinema was destroyed and under the wooden floor could be seen the tram tracks from when the building had been a tram depot. All bombed buildings had a unique smell, and since the war the smell from a building being demolished has reminded me of the Strand, though it was never quite the same.

Both All Saints Church and its hall were hit and rendered unusable. It wasn't until 1957 that restoration was completed. When Margaret and I were married there in 1956 we were the first couple to use the newly restored doorway.

Norman Drewry

Safety in the Streets

My mother, who died in 2000 in her 101st year, was in the Women's Royal Naval Service in the 1914-18 war, and was based at Immingham Docks. As a decoder she was first to know when the Zeppelins were leaving Germany to bomb our east coast. If mother was not on the last tram (10 p.m.) to leave Immingham, my grandmother knew an air raid was quite likely. When she did catch the last evening tram, Mother would leave it at the terminus at Corporation Bridge, then walk via Lock Hill, Riby Square, Cleethorpe Road and Park Street to Daubney Street where she lived. At no time, my mother recalled, was there any fear of mugging etc. as she walked home in the black-out.

Jean Ashling

Fears for our Safety

In 1944 during a bombing raid, my mother and I (a very small baby) were in our garden shelter. My sixteen-year-old brother was a messenger boy, stationed at the Town Hall and my father was on duty at Spark Street. When I was old enough to understand, my mother told me that she had feared for their safety that night.

My brother, during the butterfly bombing raid, discovered such a bomb. We have the case to this day, hung up in our garage.

Eileen Riggs

Wartime at Old Clee Farm

We were excited when the air raids began. We had to run through the farmyard to the

Anderson shelter. We heard the siren from the ARP post at Old Clee Church Hall. The sky was full of searchlight beams and gun flashes. Weelsby Hall was hit.

During one bombing raid, an incendiary set the stables on fire. We released the horses and none was hurt. My father found an army deserter in the barn. The police came and took him away. We never heard any more about him.

David Edwards

Going into the Shelter

We had an Anderson shelter in the garden at Ladysmith Road. I was only two but I remember going into it. My Grandma – who lived with us – carried me down there. The moment we heard the siren she would say, 'Come on', and grab the blankets. I always wanted the top bunk. Dad was an Air Raid Warden and he had to go on duty. While he was out he would get us fish and chips. He didn't go into the war because he had bad eyes.

Linda Oxley

Troubles with an Anderson Shelter

People with an income of less than £3.10s, were issued with a free Anderson Shelter, otherwise it cost them £5. For a while ours lay on the lawn, and consisted of six curved corrugated sheets for the sides, four straight pieces for the ends, and some angle iron. The idea was to dig a hole three feet deep and to use the soil from the hole to cover the exposed top and sides.

The man living a few doors away was the first to erect a shelter. He dug the required three-foot hole, but it kept flooding. We children of the neighbourhood really enjoyed the entertainment of watching him and his brother-in-law trying to erect the shelter. The angle iron kept disappearing into the mud, making him more and more irritable. A dozen or so local children hanging over his wall did not help. In the end he gave up, filled in the hole and gave the shelter away. When the war started he went to live and work in the comparative safety of Fleetwood.

One teatime my father announced that he intended erecting ours. He decided that to reduce the flooding he would dig the hole two foot deep. Since our neighbours' experience there had been no rain, and the two foot hole was dug. He then began erecting the shelter only to discover two parts were missing. Undaunted, Dad used a rear part for the front and filled in the gap at the rear with plywood. Then another problem arose. With the shelter being a foot higher out of the ground there was only sufficient soil for some against the sides and a little bit on top. It looked as though it was wearing a hat! My father admired his handiwork and said, "At least it's dry."

One day when I was sitting on top of it a woman walked by and said, "That shelter is all wrong. It shouldn't have wood in it and it should be covered with earth." I went into the house feeling most hurt. Eventually my father obtained the missing parts, buried it to its proper depth, fitted a wooden floor, and made a bench and a door. Of course it still flooded when it rained, but the council sent gangs round to concrete them in. Ours never flooded again, and Dad relaid the wooden floor and lined the concrete with wooden panels. He made another bench and later two wooden beds. My grandfather had two mattresses made for us.

Norman Drewry

Sharing the air-raid shelter

For a short time the Johnson's shared our shelter. Mum was not very happy about this as she did lot like Mrs Johnson. Mum said she had a nasty tongue, but as far as I could see her tongue looked the same as everybody else's. Mr Johnson must have been the original 'hen-pecked' husband. He

---

44
7-1-19.

Great Grimsby Gas Company.

JOHN TERRACE.
ENGINEER & MANAGER.
TELEPHONE No. 2432.
TELEGRAPHIC ADDRESS:
"GAS GRIMSBY."

Gas Works,
Grimsby, 31st December, 1918.

Dear Sir,

    We hereby declare that Q.M.Sgt. Jos. Taylor, No. 240092, "A" Coy., 1/5th Lincs., B.E.F., France, was in our employment before August 4th, 1914, and that we are prepared to offer him employment as Assistant Mainlayer immediately on his return to civil life.

        Yours faithfully,

        J. Perrott

Letter regarding re-employing Joseph Taylor after his service in the Great War. On the back is: 'Forwarded by the Local Advisory Committee, The Employment Exchange, Grimsby', initialled 'T.R. Secretary', and dated 2 January 1919.

was a builder's labourer, and when he came home from work she made him get changed in the outside toilet and washed at the outside tap before he was allowed into the house. He was an inoffensive man, except for his pipe – or rather what he smoked in it! The smell was dreadful. Banned from smoking in the house, he would walk up and down the garden after his tea, smoking the pipe. If it was raining he would smoke in the outside toilet.

When Mrs Johnson was in our shelter she would not stop talking, but Mr Johnson never said a word. She would tell rude jokes. I once asked Mum what they meant and she replied, "When you're older you will understand that sort of thing." When I was older and did understand that sort of thing, I had forgotten the jokes!

At length there was what Mum termed a "misunderstanding" between them, and the Johnson's then favoured another neighbour's shelter. They never again came to ours, much to my mother's relief.

Norman Drewry

CHAPTER 11
The Docks and River

The Basalt at the River Head, looking towards the Alexandra Dock.

Raising Extra Money

Once the head of the house went to sea, it was also quite normal for a lot of fishermen's wives to gather up anything of value, be it watches, clocks, clothing and bedding, etc. Then off they went to the pawnbroker's to pledge the goods. Weeks later they would recollect any pledges when the crews came back home from a trip. There were always ways of getting a few coppers pocket money. Boys would go to the well-to-do houses and knock on the backdoors. They were answered by the maid or housekeeper. The lads would volunteer to chop firewood, fill the coal scuttles, sweep pathways, polish outdoor brasses, even run errands – anything for pennies. Some were good jobs, some bad. The bad were not repeated.

Eric Robinson

A River-boat Shuffle in 1954, on board the 'Wingfield Castle' with the Riverside Jazzmen.

River Stomp

In the sixties there was a strong youth movement in the Methodist Church. The Lincoln District of the Methodist Association of Youth Clubs included Grimsby, and each year held a get-together. In 1968 the annual district event was a voyage on a hired Humber ferry paddle steamer. It sailed from New Holland Pier along the river as far as Spurn Point before returning to New Holland. The whole journey took about three hours, during which someone played records on board (later it would be called a disco). 'Waterloo Sunset' and 'Winchester Cathedral' were the favourites of the day.

I travelled to New Holland on the back of Paul's Lambretta scooter, but returned by train – using Jean's ticket, because she was on the back of Paul's scooter! Love had blossomed.

Peter Hewitt

Left: A 1938 calendar produced by fish merchant Frank Goodwin; telegrams to the company to be addressed 'Plenty, Grimsby'! The caption to this enchanting picture reads 'Anxious Moments'. The whole calendar measures 48 cm high and 27 cm wide (19 ins by 11 ins).
Right: Though the picture of this calendar has suffered some water damage, its charm remains. Issued by the Worlds Fish Supply, Ltd., it typifies a good will gesture still found today. The caption reads 'Me's good now!' Several other pre-1940 items were found among the effects of Emma Howe of Edward Street after her death in May 1982 aged 98.

An *advertisement in the Grimsby Cookery Book of 1910.*

Home from Sea

The impact of the fishing industry even affected the schools. The system in force then was that schools closed at 1 p.m. to allow the children to go home. Mothers would then go down to the docks, or to the offices of their husband's employer, to draw a percentage sub from their husband's wages. This was done every Friday, the money in subs being deducted from the settling-up pay when the trawlers next docked in port. This system would often lead to more hardship when the trawler crews came home and wanted their settling-up pay. After the wife's subs were deducted, the working crews sometimes had no money left to draw. The fishermen had been to sea – and all the hardship that entailed – for nothing. Even the miners in the coal industry did not suffer in such a manner. At least the miners could go home and have a hot bath, but on a trawler it was just not possible.

When the crews of the trawlers docked in port, the first call was to the nearest pub, or their favourite pub. Young boys would wait at the pub doors. I often saw a fisherman telling a young lad to go to his home to tell the man's wife when he would be home from the pub. Off the lad would go with the address and message, often to see an unknown lover very quickly leave the drinker's home. With a penny or two in his pocket to keep quiet, the lad was quite happy.

Eric Robinson

Pleasure Trips on the Humber

In the fifties, someone with an enterprising mind put on paddle steamer trips from the Royal Dock Basin to the lighthouse at Spurn Point. A single deck bus ran from Old Market Place to the Union Dock, where passengers alighted and then walked the length of the Royal Dock to board the steamer. The round trip to Spurn and back took about an hour and a half, but ran on summer Saturdays only. They used a spare Humber paddle steamer from the New Holland to Hull service. The journey was exciting, refreshing and very enjoyable. Other places have capitalized on their links with the sea, but rarely has Grimsby done so.

Keith Smith

Corporation Bridge raised to allow the passage of a vessel. It used to open twice a day, but only perhaps twice a year now. However, the water is cleaner and at a constant level.

Swimming in the Dock

Boys in the fifties went swimming in the River Head around the big river barges. They swam in the Alexandra Dock, around the supporting piers of the Corporation Bridge, jumping into the water off the bridge and from where the barges were tied up. They seemed to have no fear of what was below the surface of the water, nor of the murky water itself. It was not as clean as it is today, yet swimming there now is an activity that is discouraged by authorities and parents alike. It seems that today's children and youths are not interested in such an innocent activity.

Muriel Stead

Building Cold Boxes for the Pontoon

On the Pontoon 'down dock', many merchants had their own refrigerated boxes to store their fish. These boxes were three to four metres wide, around two metres deep and over two metres high. I believe the size was regulated by the Docks Board. My father worked for one of the firms that made these boxes, Link Refrigeration, run by Norman Crisp who was a refrigeration engineer. My father, Harry Leonard, together with Frank Taylor and others later, built the wooden frame, added the aluminium skin inside and out, and packed the walls, roof and floor with the insulation material. Their 'works' was at Draper's scrapyard, very close to Humber

Princess Alexandra (in hat) chatting to Doreen Phillips at the R.N.M.D.S.F. in 1981.

Princess Alexandra meeting the Bradley family at the 1981 Centenary event of the Royal National Mission to Deep Sea Fishermen. On the right (in cap) is Alex Slater, the Superintendent of the Mission.

Henry Cox and son-in-law David Bradley sheltering from the rain whilst tending the 'Penny on the plate' stall at the Royal National Mission to Deep Sea Fishermen Open Day, held on the North Wall of Number three fish dock in 1973.

Street Bridge, in a corrugated iron building that had once been a wagon repair shed. Many of those cold boxes, complete with refrigeration unit, were built by Link Refrigeration. In about 1959, a new insulating material came on to the market that improved the construction and efficiency of the pontoon boxes tremendously. I visited a local trade fair and, along with other people, was invited to lift a block of this new material. About five feet tall, three feet wide, and four inches thick (1.5 m x 1 m x 10 cm). We tensed our muscles and heaved! The large block of polystyrene leapt effortlessly into the air and we each grinned at our own embarrassment. How could such a large block weigh so little? Yet over the next few years, polystyrene revolutionized the insulation and refrigeration industry. Today we see it more frequently as an excellent packing material around electrical and delicate goods.

Even a tiny Austin mini-van was converted to a travelling cold box. Although it did not have a refrigeration unit on board to freeze the contents, the layer of polystyrene in the sides kept them sufficiently cold for local deliveries of already frozen produce. I think its registration number was PJV 1.

Brian Leonard

Well-stocked fish boxes on Grimsby's pontoon.

Working Days

In the days when the docks railway was on the map, there were always trains passing through with fish from the fish docks to all over the United Kingdom. There would always be wagons in the sidings. Spare coal from the engines was thrown on the floors, so mothers, girls and boys went to the sidings, armed with buckets or bowls or whatever, and collected any burnable coal for their homes. Even the wives of the railway police did it, so how could they stop others?

The process of work did appear to be moving on. The trams with their overhead cables for power were clanging along the town's main streets and the workforce was moving to and from work on the docks and fish curing houses. Some went on foot, but the stream of bicycles was almost as regular as any clock.

The fishing industry was showing a big improvement at this time, so the herring girls would come from as far away as Scotland every year for the herring season.

Eric Robinson

Working for a Fish Merchant

I still have vivid memories of cycling to work with my father on a fine day, about 7.00 a.m. along Bargate in the late 1950s and early 60s, with the various cherry trees in blossom. In those days cars, buses and lorries were far fewer than today. My father worked at Hewitt's Brewery and I worked for Robert Chapman Ltd, a fish merchant on the docks.

As a new boy in the office one of my

The symbol of Grimsby – the Dock Tower, built to provide hydraulic power to operate the lock gates. Reaching the top of the Dock Tower involves a long climb up a spiral staircase. However, the view is well worth it.

tasks was to take a note from a salesmen and find a particular fish buyer on the fish market and give him the note. On this note were details of the amount of fish required for the day's trade. How this worked I am not sure because I was sent out more than once. We had buyers for certain species of fish because they had become experts in the particular variety that they bought.

Another duty was going to the Fish Merchants' Association building on Fish Dock Road, to obtain the 11.00 a.m. report on the estimated vessels into Grimsby. Also listed were details of quantities and types of fish on board, which would be sold the next day. These were copied and then distributed to our buyers. If we sold any fish to other merchants, we had to make up the bills, and on Friday put them in the bill boxes which were in a building attached to the Fish Merchants' Association offices. The merchants had their own boxes and these were emptied daily. It was a type of postal service.

David Bradley

CHAPTER 12
Around Grimsby

The Town Hall from an artist's drawing. The tree, right, appears to be growing through the cobbles!

Visiting Mum's Friend

During the summer holidays my mother would take a friend and me on various trips. Often we would take the Louth bus, get off at Holton-le-Clay (which seemed a good distance anyway!), to visit my Mum's friend. She was the crossing-gate keeper and lived by the busy Grimsby-London railway line. I loved going there. Sometimes we would sit in the little waiting room, watching her open the gates for the trains. We always enjoyed taking tea with her in her quaint little cottage. It had its own scent which I found fascinating. We ate to the sound of the homely old clock ticking away. Happy Days!

Eileen Riggs

Streets Flooded

I remember clearly the floods of 1953, which affected Cleethorpes as well as Grimsby. I saw the devastation along Suggitts Lane – garden sheds marooned in the street and the road being ankle deep in sand. The railway lines had been torn up as if a giant had twisted them into strange shapes.

Doug Wise

Sunday Outings in the Car

As far as I can remember, we always had a car, and I think the neighbours thought we were rich, but our cars were mostly old ones that my Dad kept on the road by maintaining them himself. Every Sunday we would go out into the country for a ride. Croxby Pond was a place I remember well, and the other was a place we kids nicknamed 'the land of burning sands' because the sand was so dry, soft and hot that we sank down into it. There were sand-hills and grasses growing but I never did know where it was. It was definitely not the sand-hills at Humberston.

Lorna Osbourne

Bike Rides over 'The Tip'

Warm sunny Saturdays in the 1950s often meant an afternoon family outing on our bikes over Cleveland Bridge (always known locally as 'The Tip'). There was little road traffic in those days; even the occasional tramcars were more frequent than cars. Up on the bridge we could see for miles. We always stopped to watch the trains shunting below, to look at the fields towards Great Coates, and beyond them, the factories of the Humber bank. My most distinctive memory is of the smell. The smoke and steam from the engines mingled with the unique aroma of the nearby Fish Meal factory. We never knew its name, but I'm told it was Bowering's.

We would usually ride past the factories along what is now Moody Lane, Titan's (later Tioxide), and Ciba's, then through Great Coates village. There was no bypass then, so we rode along the narrow village streets, and along the road to Aylesby.

One week my back tyre blew out with a tremendous bang, putting a four inch split in it. I didn't find out what caused it. My Dad cycled back to Gilbey Road, with me on his crossbar, holding and steering my bike at his side with his left hand. Amazingly, we did not fall off.

Peter Hewitt

Getting their Sea Legs

A Humber swim was included in the attractions for Carnival Week in July 1955. The Yacht Club provided dinghies and pilots to ferry the swimmers across to Spurn Point. Some swimmers were seasick on the crossing.

Doug Wise

Beach Activities

I loved going on the trolley bus from Old Market Place to Cleethorpes. The sand pit was the usual destination, where I built sand castles for hours. I can remember the bonnets

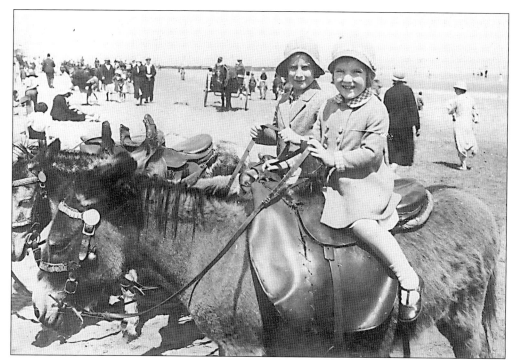

Jean and Shirley Ashling on donkeys at Cleethorpes. Were these the donkeys which were tended by Anne, Linda and Lorna?

I used to wear, with a flap at the back to keep the sun off my neck. I occasionally had a donkey ride, or a trip on a 'duck' (a DUKW, an amphibious vehicle), which took us from the pier to the water's edge when the tide was out.

Years later, I had a flight on the Auster Aircraft over Cleethorpes Beach, from the landing strip near to the Bathing Pool. It was quite an experience!

Eileen Riggs

Working the Summer at Cleethorpes

When Anne started at the Grammar School, a girl told her about the riding stables at Cleethorpes, owned by the Taskers. She went and got to know the people, Ray and Mary. It went on from there every summer. Every day we would cycle to the stables at Humber Street to collect the horses, and saddle them up, then ride them to the beach. We would run up and down the beach giving sixpenny rides all day long. Grown-ups were charged a shilling. Linda did it from the age of twelve to eighteen when she went into nursing. We became very brown and tired out.

At the end of the week we would always be paid in sixpenny pieces or threepenny bits. They weighed a ton. We had as much as a pound. We were rich but we were fit. We saved some of that.

We still see the owner. His wife was killed in a tragic riding accident on 2 or 3 September 1969. She and three children

Though the couple are not known, their dress makes this photograph interesting. Does anyone recognise them?

Mr and Mrs Cooper and friend visiting Cleethorpes' promenade, probably near to the site of Ross Castle, in the early twentieth century.

were caught in the fog and drowned.

It never rained in those days – we only remember the good times! I remember standing on the beach getting wet with horizontal rain. The horses stood with their backsides to the rain. Not a soul was on the beach, and we were waiting for the weather to come back fine again. All the people were in the arcades by then. Johnny Watkinson, Ray's right hand man, was in charge, and he would say, 'Oh, the sun will come back.'

We weren't busy on a Friday and Saturday, because on Friday the visitors bought their presents to take home, and Saturday was change-over day. We would spend a lot of time walking round finding coins. Linda found a wedding ring. She took it to the police station and left it there for the statuary time. She claimed it when nobody else did, and still has it. If it was a windy day, that was even better because the wind used to blow the top sand off. People would sit on the beach and didn't realize that coins would slip out of their pockets. We found pounds and pounds and sometimes made more money that way than we did working.

We used to love those days – it was fun down there. We kept fit and when we went back to school in the September, we'd meet up with the girls who had worked as waitresses in the cafes. They would be pale and wan-looking, and we'd go striding in as brown as berries!

Anne Harris, Linda Oxley
and Lorna Osbourne

School Trip. Class 4C of Yarborough Primary Boys' School visiting Thornton Abbey in 1963, with teacher Frank Andrews.

Lost on Cleethorpes Beach

When I was very young my sisters took me to Cleethorpes. I went to look at the donkeys near the bathing pool and soon I was lost. Strangers found me crying on the beach.

This traumatic experience had a profound effect. Whenever possible I always travel to places along familiar routes. If I have to go in unknown territory, it is vital to have a map with me otherwise I feel very insecure. Not surprisingly, I have collected dozens of maps over the years.

John D. Beasley